Advanced Styles and Insights with Midjourney

Imagine Beautiful AI Prompts

Irina Shamaeva

Apress®

Advanced Styles and Insights with Midjourney: Imagine Beautiful AI Prompts

Irina Shamaeva
El Cerrito, CA, USA

ISBN-13 (pbk): 979-8-8688-0335-2   ISBN-13 (electronic): 979-8-8688-0336-9
https://doi.org/10.1007/979-8-8688-0336-9

Managing Director, Apress Media LLC: Welmoed Spahr
Acquisitions Editor: Spandana Chatterjee
Development Editor: James Markham
Coordinating Editor: Kripa Joseph

Cover designed by eStudioCalamar

Cover image designed by Freepik (www.freepik.com)

Distributed to the book trade worldwide by Apress Media, LLC, 1 New York Plaza, New York, NY 10004, U.S.A. Phone 1-800-SPRINGER, fax (201) 348-4505, e-mail orders-ny@springer-sbm.com, or visit www.springeronline.com. Apress Media, LLC is a California LLC and the sole member (owner) is Springer Science + Business Media Finance Inc (SSBM Finance Inc). SSBM Finance Inc is a **Delaware** corporation.

For information on translations, please e-mail booktranslations@springernature.com; for reprint, paperback, or audio rights, please e-mail bookpermissions@springernature.com.

Apress titles may be purchased in bulk for academic, corporate, or promotional use. eBook versions and licenses are also available for most titles. For more information, reference our Print and eBook Bulk Sales web page at http://www.apress.com/bulk-sales.

Any source code or other supplementary material referenced by the author in this book is available to readers on GitHub (https://github.com/Apress). For more detailed information, please visit https://www.apress.com/gp/services/source-code.

If disposing of this product, please recycle the paper

Table of Contents

TABLE OF CONTENTS

About the Author

Irina Shamaeva is an AI artist at The Prompter, where lately she has been spending most of her time generating images with all available Midjourney techniques and some she has invented. She is a partner at Brain Gain Recruiting, specializing in teaching online research in application to talent sourcing. Irina is the author of a blog, BooleanStrings, which has gained 2.5 million views, and a frequent speaker at international conferences on topics like Google and LinkedIn search. Previously, Irina worked at San Francisco software start-ups and biotech firms developing software. She has an MS with Honors in Math. Irina's education and research background experience facilitate understanding and predicting complex software behavior. Irina has successfully applied these skills to navigating creative AI image-generation techniques.

Introduction

Welcome to the exploration of AI art by Midjourney, the most advanced currently available text-to-image generative artificial intelligence program and service. Give Midjourney a text picture description, and it will draw four rendered images.

Midjourney is created and hosted by the San Francisco-based independent research lab, Midjourney, Inc. It generates images from natural language descriptions, called prompts. The tool entered open beta on July 12, 2022. The service can recreate art styles, from realistic to abstract, and is recognized in the AI art community for its detailed and highly rendered images.

I started using Midjourney at version 4.0 in January 2023. Since then, there have been several versions – v 5.1, v 5.2, v 5.2R (secret version), and the current v 6.0 – with various capabilities that I will describe. Before I started using Midjourney, I could not draw. In a short time, I was creating awesome images I never could. The Facebook page where I share my art has gained over 8K followers in the year since its creation.

My book's goal is to provide a better understanding of how to craft creative prompts to achieve the desired output. This is not a Midjourney tutorial, and the book is not intended to cover all its capabilities, especially since it's a moving target. Midjourney offers two models: the default model and the Niji model. The default model is primarily what I use, and I will be focusing on it in this book. The Niji model is primarily used to create anime-style images.

This book aims to help you learn to create incredible images and styles with Midjourney and potentially other AI Image systems. I expect the readers to have started working with Midjourney and know the basics. This includes understanding how to invoke Midjourney commands and using parameters in your prompts. I will only cover concrete Midjourney version features and parameters as necessary since they change fast. (The company keeps the documentation and FAQs up to date.) Our focus will be on understanding what to expect of Midjourney when giving it this or that prompt and how to enhance and vary outcomes. I will describe the features of the drawing algorithms and how to think about prompting in a helpful way.

The more you use Midjourney, the better you'll get at steering it. It's like learning to drive – initially, you might struggle to find the right gears, but soon you'll be cruising.

I want to thank fellow AI artists who have reviewed my drafts and given valuable comments: Jade Jenerai and Valerija Mezhybovska.

My Art Before and After Midjourney

Midjourney has made a difference in my life. When an image emerging on the screen delights and satisfies you, there is a glimmer of happiness (see Figures 1 and 2)! Sharing images with friends and on social media and getting "likes" is mood-uplifting. Many Midjourney users report improved emotional health. I am confident that AI drawing tools will be used in therapy, continuing the "art therapy" approach. AI artists, including me, also use their creations for work – on blog posts, newsletters, advertisements, and social shares.

Figure 1. *Before*

Figure 2. *After*

AI Image creation has become a social adventure and a community. For me and many others, Facebook is the central hub: it has hundreds of diverse groups with shared images, prompts, ideas, and interaction. It is customary to "borrow" someone's prompt, modify it, and draw with it. "AI collective art" is happening in some of those groups.

Viewers feel a special connection if they can relate to the image. Examples are your home place, culture, favorite art style, or subject.

A reference to a long-forgotten artist, your favorite, or to an obscure computer game of your childhood that you loved makes images special. In Facebook group comments, it becomes a quick gathering of birds of a feather.

Carl Rogers once said, "What is most personal is universal." AI art is one way of realizing we are part of a community with the commonality of feelings and expressions, wherever we are in the world and whatever age. "Is AI art really art?" is a frequent topic of online debates. I support calling AI-generated images art. While AI does not have feelings, AI art evokes people's feelings. Naturally, humans react to images emotionally and personally. AI creations can make people feel the mood in a picture, to which they respond.

I am leaving out the important legal and ethical considerations regarding AI art. Others are better qualified than I am to cover the topic.

After briefly introducing Midjourney's impact on AI art, we now move to practical aspects. We'll see how different styles and syntax affect results, laying a foundation for more complex techniques discussed in later chapters. Let's start with understanding the core elements of prompt crafting in Midjourney.

CHAPTER 1

Midjourney and You

In this chapter, I describe working with Midjourney as a partnership that blends creativity with technology. I share how fine-tuning prompts turn Midjourney from a tool into a co-creator. Picture it like a kitchen crew: each word in a prompt is an ingredient, and not all get used. This analogy helps us grasp why specific prompts soar and others fall flat.

Prompt crafting is both science and art. Starting simple is a good idea. It's about guiding the AI without boxing it in, leaving room for those surprising moments of creativity. Through trial and error, we find what resonates.

Before we begin working with Midjourney, let's take a closer look at its versions.

Midjourney Versions

The latest Midjourney version is 6.0. When it came out, following nine months of development, in December of 2023, the AI drawing community realized that it significantly differs from the previous version, 5.2. Its strong side is image stylizing, and it better understands longer prompts and natural language. But it does not have the vivid imagination of version 5.2.

Important! Please do not consider v 6.0 to be superior to the previous v 5.2. Both are great at certain things, which I will outline in the following text. The prompting styles for the two versions are also different.

© The Editor(s) (if applicable) and The Author(s),
under exclusive license to APress Media, LLC, part of Springer Nature 2024
I. Shamaeva, *Advanced Styles and Insights with Midjourney*,
https://doi.org/10.1007/979-8-8688-0336-9_1

There is also a secret Midjourney version, v 5.2R. This version offers unique, sometimes unconventional, styles, expanding the creative possibilities within Midjourney.

The Best Prompt Template for v 5.2

Early in my experimentation with Midjourney versions before v 6.0, I discovered a valuable yet simple hack. If you want your image to be awesome, include "awesome" in the prompt. The output may improve even more if you use several synonyms, like "gorgeous," "wonderful," "masterpiece," "ideal," "perfect," or "contest winner." Combine several synonyms for an increasingly better effect, but don't overdo it since your scene may drown in a long prompt. Sometimes, the difference "awesome" words add is negligible; it depends on the scene.

Here is a quick example. Compare the prompts (I would prefer the second one for artistic quality):

- Wild animal photo --v 5.2 (see Figure 1-1, left)

- Gorgeous wild animal best ever photo masterpiece --v 5.2 (see Figure 1-1, right)

Figure 1-1. Wild animals – without and with adjectives

The following prompt has generated three images, which got recognition at an online image competition with mixed painting, photography, and AI submission. It was my first attempt to enter such an event. My entry ranked 5th overall out of 470 submissions from 26 countries. "masterpiece gorgeous" in the prompt has improved the outcome!

Prompt: Masterpiece gorgeous eagle full body photorealistic wildlife art, action paintings, naturecore, figurative naturalism, impressionist coloration shades --v 5.2 (see Figure 1-2)

Figure 1-2. *Wild animals*

Try the prompt with other animals instead of an eagle – a rabbit, penguin, koala, hippo, hummingbird, or anything else. The results will be excellent.

Version 6.0 does not need "beautifying" words – it does well without them.

Appendix E contains a sizable list of qualifiers for your prompts to make the images prettier. Adding them at the prompt's end might be preferable to keep the scene less affected. Feel free to experiment – the possibilities are endless!

Prompt for the images: A wonderful vase, fractured, dazzling, misty, blurry, magical, perfect, acrylic ink --v 5.2 (see Figure 1-3)

Figure 1-3. *Unusual vases*

A mix of several qualifiers has created an unusual look.

The Secret Midjourney, v 5.2R

We now have Midjourney version 6.0, which differs from v 5.2 so much. I love the imagination of 5.2; I appreciate the factual and realistic renderings of v 6.0. In addition, there is a secret version of Midjourney – I call it **v 5.2R** – which has never become official (Figure 1-4). During MJ's office hours, they once mentioned that it was the future version 5.3. (It was never released.) I wonder if this algorithm was ever intended to become a version because it is original and sometimes weird. Version 6.0 couldn't be more different.

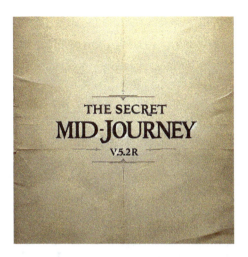

Figure 1-4. *The secret version*

There is no button or menu function to render a prompt in v 5.2R. You can do it by running Vary(Region), where you select all of a previously created image (in any version) and enter your prompt using "--v 5.2."

I encountered v 5.2R soon after Midjourney introduced the Vary(Region) function. I noticed that if I select all the images and run Vary(Region), the outcomes manifest different styles. I first called it "Midjourney Hack," then, a friend suggested calling it "Recycling."

I have recently run into a (rare) video where it is called "Secret". It suggests some applications, but I have found the use of the secret version beyond that. The algorithm is not widely known.

If your image looks unsatisfactory or dull in 5.2, try Recycling. If you want Midjourney to run its imagination wild, try Recycling. With experience, I have an intuition about the cases where it may work, but it has been hard to put it in words.

As a note, **you can start Vary(Region)/Select-All on ANY image from v 5.2**. Midjourney just goes to that secret version; the image you start with does not matter – it does not affect the outcome.

Also, Midjourney will use the secret algorithm if you select most of the image or your prompt does not relate to the original image. (If it's a smaller portion, it uses whatever version is in the prompt, 6.0 or 5.2.)

Some recent examples:

Prompt: Skin made from whimsical elements (version 5.2R, see Figure 1-5)

Figure 1-5. *Skin made from whimsical elements (5.2R)*

Prompt: A snowy landscape, each snowflake is colored, creating a mosaic on the ground, kaleidoscopic whimsical folk tale --no sun (version 5.2R, see Figure 1-6)

Figure 1-6. *Snowy landscape with mosaic*

Collaborate with AI

Some users perceive Midjourney as a hard-to-master, imperfect, and stubborn tool. A member of a Facebook Midjourney group shared their perspective: "I love MJ and use it every day, but most days I feel like I'm dealing with a disobedient child who ignores most of what I say."

But for me, Midjourney is an imaginative, intelligent, creative, and somewhat unconventional partner. It is more than a tool; I engage with it (Figure 1-7). I focus on understanding it more deeply to co-create compelling images. I'm gradually grasping the prompts Midjourney responds to effectively. This understanding develops into an intuitive skill, guiding me on what to propose.

Figure 1-7. *Midjourney and you*

My journey with Midjourney's prompting has been delightful and effortless, with some exceptions when specific requirements were involved. For instance, creating book character illustrations and images for social media for professional use and producing ordered prints have presented challenges. I recall struggling in the Midjourney v4 phase to depict a classroom with laptops, even without including people. Nonetheless, I've learned to better balance Midjourney's inventive nature and the level of detail in the prompt needed to capture the intended idea.

How Midjourney's AI Kitchen (Likely) Works

The computer has a certain amount of memory allocated for a drawing. When Midjourney reads your prompt, words take up more or less memory depending on how close they are to the beginning and how important they are for Midjourney (like "cat" is essential, "hedgehog" is less important, "a" and "the" are unimportant). When the memory limit is reached, it ignores the rest. That's why you won't see some things requested in overloaded, long prompts. You can remove other words ("tokens" in this context) if you want what's ignored in your long prompt back. When the allocated memory is exhausted, Midjourney may draw poor-quality images.

How does Midjourney read a prompt? Its code is proprietary, but it may go this way. I am no computer scientist, so please do not take the following literally, but this view helps me understand Midjourney's reactions to prompts.

With each word and word combination, a drawing AI pulls associations, or contexts, from its knowledge base, where text is connected to images. (It does not keep any text or images "as is" but has the knowledge obtained by learning.) The associations happen on several levels: the lowest level of colors and textures, then, at higher levels, styles, objects, and actions. Several software components are working in parallel on each level. It is like several cooks preparing dinner together, each with their specific role (Figure 1-8).

Figure 1-8. *Midjourney kitchen*

When the cooks are asked to make something they haven't before (like, even contradictory), they become very creative; otherwise, they may follow a recipe. The creative work is called "zero-shot learning" in AI.

In AI image creation, zero-shot learning means the AI can make images of things it has never learned explicitly about. Midjourney can generate pictures of things it hasn't seen before. Contradictory prompts combining things, qualities, and actions that have never been depicted together can have fantastic results!

Compared to cooks, AI drawing compares the results with the request and may redo the image-making several times.

Prompts and Styles

Crafting effective prompts for Midjourney itself requires artistic skills. The key lies in striking a balance between being specific enough to guide the AI and leaving enough open-endedness to allow for creative surprises and styles.

The choice of words, their arrangement, and the concepts they convey influence the outcome. This section offers practical tips for mastering the art of prompt crafting to yield the most compelling and relevant results.

Midjourney has documentation on its website and more in Discord's FAQs. However, no amount of writing or videos would constitute "complete" documentation for an AI drawing system due to its "black box" nature. Experimentation is critical in learning AI Image art – or any AI modality. I sincerely hope that the book will become your experimentation companion and guide.

Midjourney text prompts have a particular syntax consisting of words and parameters. We will review the parameters later and only use "pure text" prompts now.

Prompts and Series of Images As AI Art Form

Sometimes, your goal is to create one image, for example, for your social profile banner or to print on canvas. But for many applications and social shares, AI artists create not one but a series of images from the same prompt. In this context, a prompt and several images generated from it become the creation within the audience of people who appreciate AI art. Short or unusual prompts with captivating results attract special attention.

"Cup couple" is a two-word prompt that produces a variety of images. The simplicity of the prompt is part of the attraction (see Figures 1-9 and 1-10 for examples).

Figure 1-9. *Cup couple, version 5.2*

Figure 1-10. Mona Chameleona, Renaissance, version 6.0

A share on Facebook received a comment: "Is not so funny the result as the prompt."

Be Brief, Unless Your Scene Is Complex

Short prompts are your friends if you are starting out (or in any case!). Longer prompts may confuse Midjourney, resulting in so-so results.

Compare a prompt I copied online and ran in both versions:

Beautiful woman Amazon warrior, long red hair, gold armor, cinematic, hyper-detailed, insane details, beautifully color graded, unreal engine, DOF, super-resolution, megapixel, cinematic lightning, anti-aliasing, FKAA, TXAA, RTX, SSAO, post processing, post production, tone mapping, CGI, VFX, SFX, insanely detailed and intricate, hyper maximalist, hyper-realistic, volumetric, photorealistic, ultra photoreal, ultra-detailed, intricate details, 8K, super detailed, full color, volumetric lightning, HDR, realistic, unreal engine, 16K, sharp focus, stylized acrylic --v 5.2 (see Figure 1-11)

Figure 1-11. *Beautiful woman Amazon warrior, long prompt, version 5.2*

Beautiful woman Amazon warrior, long red hair, gold armor, cinematic, hyper-detailed, insane details, beautifully color graded, unreal engine, DOF, super-resolution, megapixel, cinematic lightning, anti-aliasing, FKAA, TXAA, RTX, SSAO, post processing, post production, tone mapping, CGI, VFX, SFX, insanely detailed and intricate, hyper maximalist, hyper-realistic, volumetric, photorealistic, ultra photoreal, ultra-detailed, intricate details, 8K, super detailed, full color, volumetric lightning, HDR, realistic, unreal engine, 16K, sharp focus, stylized acrylic --v 6.0 (see Figure 1-12)

Figure 1-12. *Beautiful woman Amazon warrior, long prompt,*
version 6.0

Prompt: Woman Amazon warrior, long red hair, gold armor, stylized
acrylic --v 5.2 (see Figure 1-13)

Figure 1-13. *Woman Amazon warrior, version 5.2*

Prompt: Woman Amazon warrior, long red hair, gold armor, stylized acrylic --v 6.0 (see Figure 1-14)

Figure 1-14. *Woman Amazon warrior, version 6.0*

A battery of "qualifiers" does not always add quality.

What to Draw? Debugging the Output

In the initial exploration mode, combine only a few subjects or actions in a prompt. If you run a long and complex prompt, you may overwhelm Midjourney, and it will ignore part of your prompt or draw something messy. Instead, go with simple scenes and add stylizing words to your prompt. Throughout the book, you will see many examples where a brief scene description and a list of qualities work well.

You can look for ideas everywhere – around you, on social media, in movies and books, in your dreams or memories. Draw different cultures, historical periods, or abstract concepts like emotions or weather conditions. Midjourney "knows" about many photographers, architects, sculptors, painters, artistic styles, and drawing and painting media.

If you are looking to draw something specific – either for an application such as to accompany your professional blog, to send a greeting card, or for your enjoyment – your task will get increasingly more challenging with the number of requirements.

Midjourney is terrific at some subjects and styles but only at some. While Midjourney can draw a perfect, detailed medieval portrait, the wrong number of fingers and weird hand gestures are common even on simple drawings. For further considerations, check out the "Limitations" section.

Prompts rarely produce satisfactory results at first. When you have an idea and enter your prompt guess into Midjourney, you will notice flaws to correct or styles and subjects to alter for better outcomes. Drawing in AI is iterating and refining your input until the images fit your liking.

You can also use prompt results as a creative springboard. For example, you may add characters or change the scene from rural to urban and keep the style.

Aspects of Image Prompting

To enhance your AI-generated images, consider these refined strategies, drawing inspiration from specific examples:

- Use a range of themes, from the whimsical ("a garden of bioluminescent flowers") to the historic ("Old English town, cobbled streets"). Experiment with styles like "oil pastel" or "watercolor ink" for varied artistic effects.

- Add imaginative details. For instance, "a hippo, warmly dressed" or "a dragon with patchwork Maori patterns."

- Use specific artistic techniques in your prompts. Mention "chiaroscuro" for dramatic light and shadow effects or "stippling" for a dotted, texture-rich appearance.

- Infuse your prompts with emotional or sensory words, for example, "romantic candlelit dinner" or "tranquil early spring landscape."

- Incorporate cultural or historical aspects. References like "Egyptian pyramids in hieroglyphic style" or "roaring 20s fashion" add a layer of richness and context to your images.

- Blend fantastical elements with realistic details, such as "animals in human attire" or "surreal landscapes with real town elements." This fusion creates intriguing, multilayered artwork.

- Challenge the AI's capabilities with controversial, creative prompts. Test its limits with innovative concepts like "abstract Braille flowers" or "architecture stitched with the Eiffel Tower and London Bridge."

Summary

Midjourney version 6.0 is adept at stylizing images and parsing longer prompts, whereas 5.2 shines with its creative flair, and 5.2R has a wild imagination. I advise against considering one version outright better; each serves different artistic needs.

To wrap up, the essence of this chapter is experimentation. Each attempt with Midjourney teaches us more about the dance of words and imagery, pushing us toward more nuanced, compelling creations. Let's keep exploring, refining our prompts, and watching the art unfold.

Chapter 2 focuses on creating effective prompts for Midjourney, pointing out its unique approach to understanding prompts, which differs from simple English.

CHAPTER 2

Gauging the Effectiveness of Midjourney's Prompts

This chapter dives into Midjourney's prompt language, showing how to communicate effectively with the AI to create images. It explains the role of prompt length, word order, and specific word repetition in influencing image outcomes. The chapter reveals that certain words have "internal weights," affecting the focus of image generation. Short prompts tend to produce more imaginative results. Including artist names or styles in prompts guides the AI toward specific aesthetics. I also cover using multi-prompts and style parameters to refine results and discuss the AI's limitations in accurately depicting complex subjects.

Prompts Are *Not* in English: They Are in MJEnglish

Midjourney has been trained on a gigantic dataset of images and associated words and phrases. Given a prompt, it navigates to the parts of its knowledge for content relevant to the words ("tokens") in the prompt and pulls out colors, styles, and objects from its storage to form the newly created image.

© The Editor(s) (if applicable) and The Author(s),
under exclusive license to APress Media, LLC, part of Springer Nature 2024
I. Shamaeva, *Advanced Styles and Insights with Midjourney*,
https://doi.org/10.1007/979-8-8688-0336-9_2

When beginner AI artists describe complex, detailed visual scenes in a long English paragraph as they would to another person, the outcomes are often uninteresting or messy. Keep in mind: your audience is not human! However, long, logical descriptions like quotations from poems and stories work fine.

Prompt: I wandered lonely as a cloud that floats on high o'er vales and hills, when all at once I saw a crowd, a host, of golden daffodils; beside the lake, beneath the trees, fluttering and dancing in the breeze. Continuous as the stars that shine and twinkle on the Milky Way, they stretched in never-ending line along the margin of a bay: Ten thousand saw I at a glance, tossing their heads in sprightly dance. --v 5.2 (see Figure 2-1)

Figure 2-1. *Lake Poem, v 5.2*

Prompt: I wandered lonely as a cloud that floats on high o'er vales and hills, when all at once I saw a crowd, a host, of golden daffodils; beside the lake, beneath the trees, fluttering and dancing in the breeze. Continuous as the stars that shine and twinkle on the Milky Way, they stretched in never-ending line along the margin of a bay: Ten thousand saw I at a glance, Tossing their heads in sprightly dance. --v 6.0 (see Figure 2-2)

Figure 2-2. *Lake Poem, v 6.0*

Let us look into various aspects of the Midjourney prompt processing approach.

If the prompt is long and rich with different subjects, MJ may ignore what it says at the end – it will not draw it in an obvious way.

The word order matters – words at the beginning matter more. The altered word order somewhat changes the output even if the prompt meaning stays unchanged. Repeating a word in v 5.2 (called the "cowbelling" technique) will give it more importance.

While words carry different levels of influence on the image, everything in the prompt may affect its output – even punctuation marks. Articles "a" and "the" and punctuation like commas all slightly influence the output. An added color may convert the output from realistic to stylized.

Short prompts in Midjourney often generate more attractive images because Midjourney applies its extraordinary imagination to interpret and create extra elements or style for the image.

Words (tokens) have internal weights in Midjourney. These are not numbers we can get hold of, but rather observed keyword behavior when included in prompts. Of two subjects in a prompt, the higher-weight one may take over the scene. Cat, woman, umbrella, and mushroom are some of the most influential words, that is, the highest-weight tokens. The weights are "high" because MJ's training data was full of those subjects – because they are so popular on the Internet.

The influencer words and associated content get priority. If you draw a cat (high internal weight) and a hedgehog (low internal weight), you will likely get a few cats and no hedgehogs. We will discuss ways to work with the prompt to bring the hedgehogs back into the scene.

If Midjourney v 5.2 does not understand what you want to create, it will draw a beautiful woman with long, wavy hair. Type a random character sequence, and you will get her image. Other default outputs are floating castles and mushrooms. There is no reason to be proud of these images!

When the prompt is unclear, MJ draws high-weight tokens, such as a woman, cat, or mushrooms (see Figure 2-3).

Figure 2-3. *Default image, v 5.2*

MJ v 6.0 may also draw a woman, usually Asian, though its choices are more expansive (see Figure 2-4).

Figure 2-4. *Default image, v 6.0*

Midjourney supports multi-prompts, where double colons and assigned weights separate prompt parts. A particular case is negative weights for excluding words. A negative-weight word takes with it the associated part of the image base, which does not then participate in the image creation. Naturally, it is harder to predict or control the outputs of prompts with words excluded.

Midjourney has style parameters that affect the output. There is a default style, a "Niji" model, and a "raw" style. The "raw" style uses the least of Midjourney's interpreting and beautifying algorithms. Outcomes of the style raw are more realistic.

Midjourney has associations with every word you might use in a prompt. Rain in a prompt can bring up an umbrella, beautiful – a woman. Midjourney may process and render your prompts in a surprising fashion, riding on its associations. If it is unclear what brought specific features to an image from its prompt, slightly alter the prompt, and you may get an insight.

Character and Color Confusion

Midjourney understands natural language, but only to a certain extent. Without specific prompt language to discern the characters, it may mix up your characters, their qualities, and colors.

Consider the prompt: green aliens meet pink frogs. In English, there is no ambiguity. But let us look at a collection that Midjourney produced. Since I did not have the exact goal of aliens meeting frogs, I was satisfied with these:

Prompt: Green aliens meet pink frogs --v 5.2 (see Figure 2-5)

Figure 2-5. *Green aliens meet pink frogs --v 5.2*

Version 6.0 does a somewhat better job, but not entirely:
Prompt: Green aliens meet pink frogs --v 6.0 (see Figure 2-6)

Figure 2-6. *Green aliens meet pink frogs --v 6.0*

Include Artists and Photographers in Prompts

You can combine any scene with an artist's name or several names. Drawing something an artist never has can be entertaining!

Prompt: Out of order washing machine, Renoir --v 5.2 has generated these four amusing images (see Figure 2-7).

Figure 2-7. *Out of order washing machine, Renoir --v 5.2*

Here is another example.

Prompt: A self-portrait by {Vincent van Gogh, Frida Kahlo, Jackson Pollock, Claude Monet, Georgia O'Keeffe, Salvador Dalí, Rembrandt van Rijn, Wassily Kandinsky} --v 6.0 (see Figure 2-8)

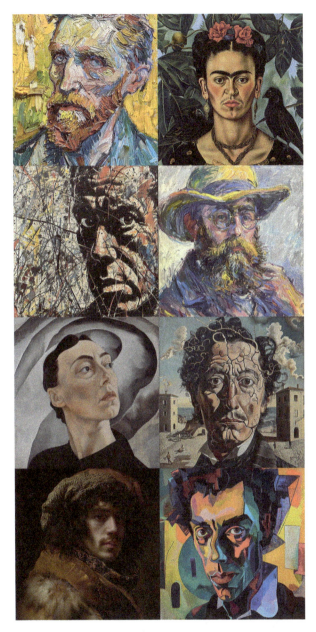

Figure 2-8. *Self-portraits*

(In Midjourney's syntax, including a series of phrases separated by commas in curly brackets makes it run the prompt for each item. It is called permutations.)

Interesting images come from mixing artists' styles. Here is an example.

Prompt: Ancient Greek Mexican rococo starry nights by Matisse --v 5.2 (see Figure 2-9)

Figure 2-9. *Mixing styles*

In Appendix C, you will find sample prompts to render images in many prominent artists' styles.

Include Drawing Styles in Prompts

Here are a few examples of Midjourney responding to the specified style names and qualities. My prompt includes three existing and one made-up style. It is up to Midjourney how to interpret the nonexistent word "bioluminuscent." (As I mentioned, using a sequence in {} generates a series of images with each item from the sequence.)

Prompt: Tiny house {outsider, bioluminuscent, ebru, encaustic} art --v 6.0 (see Figure 2-10)

Figure 2-10. *Tiny house in various styles*

You will find a sample list of styles in Appendix A.

Set a Tone for the Scene

Besides physical descriptions, adding mood or atmospheric elements to prompts would significantly change the outcome. For example, "peaceful" or "mysterious" can set a tone for the scene. See how rural landscape looks differently depending on the style qualifier applied:

Prompt: {Peaceful, mysterious, lonely, charming} Dutch rural landscape --v 6.0 (see Figure 2-11)

Figure 2-11. *Setting a tone for the scene*

You will find a sample list of qualifiers (or modifiers) in Appendix E.

Limitations

Midjourney is creative and attuned to beauty. However, there are some subjects that Midjourney won't manage well in its current versions. Challenging subjects include hands, arms, legs, and scissors, to name a few. These are problematic for all AI drawing tools to various extents.

Prompt: The best scissor set for cloth on display --v 5.2 (see Figure 2-12)

Figure 2-12. *Scissors (v 5.2)*

Prompt: The best scissor set for cloth on display --v 6.0 (see Figure 2-13)

Figure 2-13. *Scissors (v 6.0)*

Midjourney has a rich vocabulary but may not know some words, like Latin plant names or some artists' styles. If a word is not in its vocabulary, it may cook up something interesting. (The same goes for misspelled and nonsense words.)

Midjourney cannot draw your portrait with likeness unless you are a celebrity like Maggie Smith or Idris Elba.

Summary

In this chapter, we have covered the following:

- The necessity for clear, logical descriptions to enhance image outcomes

- How the length of a prompt, the sequence of words, and repetition ("cowbelling") influence the final image

- Certain words' "internal weights" significance in determining image content

- Short prompts, which usually lead to more imaginative outputs because of Midjourney's interpretative process

- Adding artist names or styles directing the AI toward specific aesthetics

- Employing multi-prompts and style parameters to refine results, though Midjourney might resort to default images with ambiguous prompts

- Recognized challenges in depicting complex subjects or precise artistic styles, with advice for effective prompt formulation

In Chapter 3, we will review various ways to use images and text prompts.

CHAPTER 3

Using Existing Images As Your Base (Multimedia Prompts)

Surprise! Midjourney is not just a text-to-image tool. It is much more.

You can use existing images in addition to text as part of a prompt. Creating an image with mixed text-and-image input may take several Midjourney runs. The "prompt" here is no longer text but a sequence of inputs, including text and images. We don't have a language to describe it, and it may be hard to reproduce due to the output variability at each step.

Midjourney offers several functions to generate an image based on one already created.

If you use the same prompt, Vary(Strong) and Vary(Subtle) develop variations of your image. This can be helpful if you like the composition and style but not a specific implementation. If you use a different prompt, however, the creation will have visual elements from both the original image and the prompt.

© The Editor(s) (if applicable) and The Author(s),
under exclusive license to APress Media, LLC, part of Springer Nature 2024
I. Shamaeva, *Advanced Styles and Insights with Midjourney*,
https://doi.org/10.1007/979-8-8688-0336-9_3

Vary(Subtle)

You can use Vary(Subtle) with a slightly changed prompt to create different versions of the same object.

Prompt: A non-existent elegant bright flat colors chess figure --v 6.0 (see Figure 3-1)

Figure 3-1. *Chess figure*

Vary(Subtle) with the prompt: Chess figure made of color noble marble --v 6.0 (see Figure 3-2)

Figure 3-2. *Chess figure variation*

Vary(Subtle) with the prompt: Seamless mahogany chess figure --v 6.0 (see Figure 3-3)

Figure 3-3. *Chess figure variation*

Here is another example:

First image prompt: A portrait of a six-year-old boy with short brown curly hair, green eyes, reading glasses, curious face --no freckles --v 6.0 (see Figure 3-4)

Figure 3-4. *Six-year-old boy*

The rest are done with Vary(Subtle), using the same prompt, but growing ages and replacing "boy" with "man" at age 18 (see Figure 3-5).

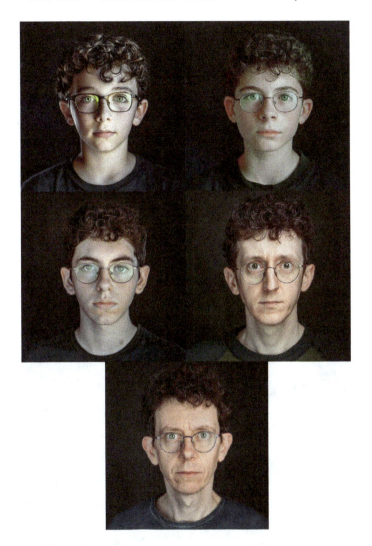

Figure 3-5. *Growing ages*

Vary(Subtle) works "at the pixel level." It does not know the image content but follows the colors and lines. It is supposed to be used with prompts that are alike. But in the following, I used Vary(Subtle) with a different prompt. It is hard for Midjourney to figure out what to do with Subtle; results are all over the place, but many are interesting.

Prompt: Starry swirly lines backdrop --v 6.0 (see Figure 3-6)

Figure 3-6. *Starry swirly lines backdrop*

Vary(Subtle) over the images (Figure 3-6); prompt: elegant tea set, England 1850s --v 6.0 (see Figure 3-7)

Figure 3-7. *Elegant tea set, Vary(Subtle)*

Vary(Strong). Remixing with the Prompt Change

Running the same prompt with Vary(Strong) will create variations of your existing image. But you can also remix and change the prompt. In this case, Vary(Strong) "absorbs" the artistic style of the original image. One technique utilizing Vary(Strong) is to draw an abstract background that will become material for "making" things such as dishes or dresses. After you have created the background image, select Vary(Strong) and enter a new prompt. For the example, I used the same images as for Vary(Subtle) shown previously (Figure 3-6).

Prompt for the background: Starry swirly lines backdrop --v 6.0 (see Figure 3-6)

Vary(Strong), prompt: Elegant tea set, England 1850s --v 6.0 (see Figure 3-8)

Figure 3-8. *Elegant tea set, Vary(Strong)*

Prompt: Giant tiger, stained glass --v 6.0 (see Figure 3-9)

Figure 3-9. *Giant tiger, stained glass*

Vary(Strong) with the image, prompt: yellow cobbled road in Africa, rain --v 6.0 (see Figure 3-10)

Figure 3-10. *Cobbled road in Africa*

Vary(Region)

The third function, Vary(Region), allows you to select areas within a painting to redraw, optionally, with a new prompt. It is an excellent way to fix the "wrong" hands and other elements.

Prompt: Decoupage lady, 1920s fashion, cartoon painting, spectacular --v 6.0 --w 20 --style raw (Figure 3-11)

Figure 3-11. *Decoupage lady, foot backward*

Using Vary(Region) with the same prompt (Figure 3-12)

Figure 3-12. Vary(Region)

I fixed the wrong-pointing foot (Figure 3-13).

Figure 3-13. Decoupage lady, feet OK

You can also draw a room or a road, select an area in the image, and then start populating the selected area with something new to the scene.

Prompt: A dirt road in a remote California desert location, spring, bloom, cloudy, pretty clouds --v 6.0 (see Figure 3-14)

Figure 3-14. *Empty road*

Vary(Region) of the image (Figure 3-15) with prompt: A giant clever rabbit in a hurry --v 6.0 (see Figure 3-16)

Figure 3-15. *A road with a rabbit*

Vary(Region) of the image (Figure 3-14) with prompt: A welcoming lemonade stand --v 6.0 (see Figure 3-16)

Figure 3-16. *A road with a lemonade stand*

Vary(Region) of the image (Figure 3-14) with prompt: a new swimming pool --v 6.0 (see Figure 3-17)

Figure 3-17. *A road with a swimming pool*

Image Reference, --sref

You can also refer to an existing image, called a "reference" image, with the parameter --sref. It is one of the newer functions that I love! The format is --sref <URL of an image>. You can specify one of the four available flavors with the parameter --sv: --sv 1, --sv 2, --sv 3, and --sv 4. If not specified, the value is --sv 4 (which I used).

Example. The reference image prompt: there is a house in the mouse, bold colors --v 6.0 --style raw (see Figure 3-18)

Figure 3-18. *"A house in the mouse," prompt for the reference image*

Prompt: The secret club of introverted sheep --sref <URL of the ref image> --v 6.0 --style raw

produces these (see Figure 3-19).

Figure 3-19. *Introverted sheep*

Here is another example.

Reference image prompt: An antique jewelry box with filigree detailing, open to reveal velvet-lined compartments filled with vintage jewels, mesmerizing acrylic watercolor, clean ink contours --v 6.0 (see Figure 3-20)

Figure 3-20. *Antique jewelry box*

Prompt: Idyllic farm, early spring, bold colors --sref <URL of the ref image> --v 6.0 --s 500 (see Figure 3-21)

Figure 3-21. *Idyllic farm*

Here is a demonstration of each of the four ways to use an image in a prompt we have covered.

Reference image prompt (with an intentional typo): Exotic fliora --v 6.0 --c 20 (see Figure 3-22)

Figure 3-22. *Exotic "fliora"*

1) The first way is to include a public URL of the image in the prompt. In the example, I use the URL of the image I generated (Figure 3-23). But generally, you can upload any image to Discord or the Midjourney site and use its URL.

Prompt: <URL of the ref image> a meadow --v 6.0 (see Figure 3-23)

Figure 3-23. *A meadow (with an image prompt)*

Figure 3-24. *A meadow with Vary(Subtle)*

2) Run Vary(Subtle) with a new prompt over the image (Figure 3-23). Prompt: A meadow --v 6.0 (see Figure 3-25)

3) Run Vary(Strong) with the prompt over the image (Figure 3-22). Prompt: A meadow --v 6.0 (see Figure 3-25)

Figure 3-25. *A meadow with Vary(Strong)*

4) Make the image (Figure 3-22) a style reference. Prompt: A meadow --sref <URL of the ref image> --v 6.0 (see Figure 3-26)

Figure 3-26. *A meadow with style reference*

Summary

To summarize, functions combining text and images include the following:

- Vary(Subtle) and Vary(Strong): Modify an existing image, based on the same or a new prompt, helpful for adjustments or adding new elements.

- Vary(Region): Redraws specific parts of an image, perfect for populating scenes with new details or characters or making adjustments.

- Prompt with a reference image by including its URL; helps to draw, for example, a subject that Midjourney is not familiar with.

- --sref parameter: Incorporates an existing image's style via a URL into your prompt.

These features underscore Midjourney's versatility in creating detailed, customized images through textual and visual prompts. One of the latest Midjourney additions is "character references," invoked by "--cref <image>" in the prompt. It is a way to draw the same person or character depicted in <image> in various situations. I will cover it in Chapter 6.

The next chapter delves deeper into Midjourney's capabilities.

CHAPTER 4

Advanced Midjourney Capabilities

This chapter focuses on refining your Midjourney images with advanced techniques and provides tools for precise control over your image's final look, turning basic prompts into detailed visual stories. It covers the following topics:

- Multi-prompts: Combining ideas with double colons and adjusting their influence through weights

- Negative weights: Fine-tuning by emphasizing or reducing specific elements

- Upscaling (version 6.0): Enhancing image quality for more detailed outcomes

- Style parameters: Adjusting chaos and weirdness levels to influence the image's style

- Pan and zoom: Controlling the framing of your image for precise compositions

- Controlling contrasting characters in v 6.0

- Text and limitations

- Midjourney troubleshooting

- Creating logos

Multi-prompts

Separating parts of your prompt with double colons is called multi-prompting. Midjourney processes each sub-prompt separately and then negotiates the final image. Multi-prompts have weights affecting how strongly each part of the prompt should influence the outcome. Place the weight after the double colon. A weight applies to the preceding part of the prompt (not just to the last word).

It is unclear how multi-prompting works in v 6.0; I will describe what it does in v 5.2.

Examples:

dark bluebells::10 light roses::70 --v 5.2 (see Figure 4-1)

dark bluebells::50 light roses::33 --v 5.2 (see Figure 4-1)

Figure 4-1. *Bluebells or roses*

Due to the weights, the first image shows roses, and the second shows bluebells. By manipulating the weights, we can create a balance between the flowers, resulting in "bluebell-roses." We call this "the tipping point."

Prompt: Dark bluebells::50 light roses::33 --v 5.2 (see Figure 4-2)

Figure 4-2. *"Bluebell-roses"*

Being Negative

You can use negative weights in a multi-prompt. Midjourney's syntax "--no <keyword>" is the same as "<keyword>::-0.5" given that the default weight is 1. For simplicity, I use round numbers for weights; what matters is the ratios of the weights within a prompt. That is, these prompts are similar:

- Something --no other

- Something::1 other::-0.5

- Something:100 other::-50

Giving a word like "tiger" a negative weight does not guarantee that you will see no tigers in the image. They may still appear if your prompt hints at tigers' habitat or actions, but Midjourney will do its best to avoid tigers.

Example: Before I added "zebra" with a negative weight of -10, I mostly got zebras, as Midjourney's association with barcodes and nature. With -10, I still got a zebra, but also others:

Prompt: Nature's barcode masterpiece::100 zebra::-10 --s 50 --v 5.2 (see Figure 4-3)

Figure 4-3. *Nature's barcode*

With a strong zebra exclusion, I have lost not only zebras but barcodes as well:

Prompt: Nature's barcode masterpiece::100 zebra::-99 --s 50 --v 5.2 (see Figure 4-4)

Figure 4-4. *Nature's barcode, strong zebra exception*

Just like including a word in Midjourney brings in associations (e.g., rain ~ umbrella), excluding a word using a negative weight removes the associated visuals. A higher weight ratio will exclude a token "even more," changing the style.

In v 5.2, I use exclusions often. Images with excluded suns, moons, mushrooms, or persons often look original and exciting.

Compare the results of these prompts. I find the second image, with the sun excluded, more attractive.

Note that the weight applies to all preceding words. For example, in the second prompt, "quilt field" has a weight of 100.

Prompts: Quilt field --v 5.2; quilt field::100 sun::-80 --v 5.2 (see Figure 4-5)

Figure 4-5. *Quilt field with and without the sun (v 5.2)*

Results can be appealing but sometimes more challenging to explain than in the preceding example with the sun exclusion.

However, "heavy" exclusions may also negatively affect your output and make it less attractive. It happens with the same prompt in v 6.0. Though none of the images shows the sun, its exclusion leads to duller images.

Prompt: Quilt field --v 6.0 (see Figure 4-6)

Figure 4-6. *Quilt field (v 6.0, sun included)*

Prompt: Quilt field::100 sun::-80 --v 6.0 (see Figure 4-7)

Figure 4-7. *Quilt field (v 6.0, sun excluded)*

In v 5.2, you can include and exclude the same word with positive and negative weights – they will not cancel each other out but may show associations with the word vs. its direct renderings. Strong words like "cat" may still "make it" into the images.

Prompt: Whoo-hoo cat::10000 cat::-9999 --v 5.2 --s 400 (see Figure 4-8)

Figure 4-8. *Whoo-hoo cat*

I highly recommend playing with negative weights!

Upscaling in v 6.0

In Midjourney v 6.0, the results of the U button are *not* the "final" images, even though many of us enjoy and share them. For the final image(s), where Midjourney "is done," you need to use the Upscale(Subtle) or Upscale(Creative) button. Upscaled images may look different. Midjourney is not just upscaling like other tools; see in the following how the examples differ from the original. The subtle upscale has added image clarity; the creative has added tears. (This was not the case in v 5.2.)

Example:

1) Result of "U" (see Figure 4-9)

Figure 4-9. *Original image*

2) Subtle upscale (see Figure 4-10)

Figure 4-10. *Subtle upscale*

3)   Creative upscale (see Figure 4-11)

Figure 4-11. *Creative upscale*

Midjourney Styles and Aesthetic Parameters

Midjourney responds to these styles, communicated in your prompt by the --style parameter:

Default (nothing to add)

--style raw (weak influence of the beautifying algorithms)

Midjourney also has a "Niji" model, which I consider more of a style. It is evoked if you write --niji as part of your prompt. Alternatively, you can switch the model in your settings command to "Niji 5" or "Niji 6".

With a bit of messed-up terminology, Midjourney also has a "stylize" parameter – a number telling the AI with what "strength" to apply the style. The syntax is --s <number>. The number ranges from 0 to 1000.

So, for example, prompt "windy weather in Kansas --style raw --s 1000" is about the style raw applied with a large weight of 1000. Style raw with a high style and default style with a low --s value are both candidates for images that more precisely reflect your prompt.

Examples demonstrating styles and style influences:

Prompt: Windy weather in Kansas --style raw --s 1000 --v 6.0 (see Figure 4-12)

Figure 4-12. *Windy weather in Kansas --style raw*

Prompt: Windy weather in Kansas --niji 6 --s 250 (see Figure 4-13)

Figure 4-13. *Windy weather in Kansas --niji*

Prompt: Windy weather in Kansas --s 0 --v 6.0 (see Figure 4-14)

Figure 4-14. *Windy weather in Kansas --v 6.0, no styling*

Prompt: Windy weather in Kansas --s 1000 --v 6.0 (see Figure 4-15)

Figure 4-15. *Windy weather in Kansas --v 6.0, maximum styling*

The parameter --c is called "chaos" in Discord and "variety" on the Midjourney website. The syntax is --c <number>. Low chaos values offer more repeatable results, and higher values – more variety. I like setting the value at 10.

The parameter --w stands for weirdness, and the value goes from 0 to 3000. If you set --w higher than zero, your images would become odd-looking, unexpected. Depending on the prompt, you may see some strangeness in style even at a low --w, like 2 or 3. As an experiment, I have created a "maximum" weird image with the prompt X --w 3000 --s 50 --v 6.0 --style raw (see Figure 4-16).

Figure 4-16. *Maximum wierdness*

Additional "extreme" examples:

A cafe in Lyon --w 3000 --s 50 --v 6.0 --style raw (see Figure 4-17)

Figure 4-17. *Maximum wierdness, cafe in Lyon*

A Middle Ages village --w 3000 --s 500 --c 10 --v 6.0 (see Figure 4-18)

Figure 4-18. *Maximum wierdness, Middle Ages village*

Pan and Zoom

Pan and Zoom allow you to expand the image to the right, left, up, down, and in all directions. Midjourney will imagine what lies beyond the drawing.

Example prompt: My entire collection of contrasting designer purses on the wall display --v 5.2

I zoomed out several times (see Figure 4-19).

Figure 4-19. *Zoom out, designer purses collection*

If you choose Pan or "custom zoom," you can change the prompt. Note that the changed prompt will only influence the extended part.

Example:

Prompt: A portrait of a 6-year-old naive girl Peggy with short light curly hair, blue eyes, wearing a summer hat and silk scarf --no freckles --v 6.0 (see Figure 4-20)

Figure 4-20. *Peggy*

I panned right and left with "2 portraits of" and then "3 portraits of," adding "profile view" (see Figure 4-21).

Figure 4-21. *Pan left and right, Peggy and her sisters*

Tip   If you keep the prompt and change the --c or --s value, you will get look-alikes in one or more of the four images. (At some --c or --s value, MJ will switch to another "person" and will again last for a range of values.) Use the same seed.

Prompt: A color pencil portrait of a 40-year-old man from the Republic of Georgia --seed 898 --v 6.0 --c <varied from 5 to 45> --s <varied from 60 to 400> (see Figure 4-22)

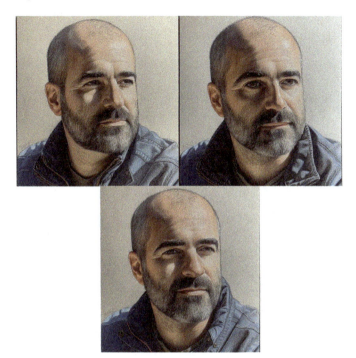

Figure 4-22. *Man from the Republic of Georgia*

Controlling Contrasting Characters in v 6.0

Version 6.0 is more attuned to natural language than the previous versions of Midjourney. However, the language it understands when drawing images with various characters is specific. You can draw different characters without Midjourney mixing them up (in most images) by doing the following. The first prompt sentence needs to set the scene and characters. The following sentences need to refer to the characters named in the first sentence. As long as the reference phrases follow, the character names can be anything.

Example prompt: 5 and 8 are having a tea party. 5 is a woman librarian. 8 is a fearless bunny --v 6.0 --style raw (see Figure 4-23)

Figure 4-23. *A librarian and a bunny*

Another example prompt: Three different men stand together, talking. The man on the right is dark and wearing glasses. The man in the middle is a hippo, warmly dressed. The man on the left is in overalls with blue eyes. Quiet countryside. --v 6.0 (see Figure 4-24)

Figure 4-24. *Three different characters, countryside*

Prompt: Three deks sit on a wooden bench, the dek on the right is a charming grandma, knitting. The dek in the middle is Darth Vader, friendly; the dek on the left is a cloud with blue eyes. Peaceful oil, impasto --v 6.0 (see Figure 4-25)

Figure 4-25. *Three different characters on a bench*

Text in v 6.0

Version 6.0 can write text, but its capabilities are limited. With long text or uncommon words, expect misspellings in the rendering, often written in tiny letters. The trick to writing text is to put the text in quotation marks inside the prompt. You can repeat parts of the starting phrase in a multi-prompt to reinforce it. You can say that the text is "bold," "large," or "prominent" to make it stand out. Note that Midjourney also uses the words in quotation marks as part of the prompt.

Example prompt: Image, write text "Prompt, please!" --v 6.0 --style raw --s 50 (see Figure 4-26)

Figure 4-26. *"Prompt, please!"*

Another example prompt: Lewis Carroll's text "Alice's Adventures in Wonderland" is a whimsical and imaginative tale that transcends its apparent simplicity:: text "Alice's Adventures in Wonderland" is a whimsical and imaginative tale --v 6.0 --s 70 --style raw (see Figure 4-27)

Figure 4-27. *"Alice's Adventures in Wonderland"*

The following series demonstrates how Midjourney includes the text you put in quotes as part of what to draw.

Prompt: Text "<what it says>" on the elegant artsy lithography classic tarot card --ar 9:16 --v 6.0 --style raw --s 50 (see Figure 4-28)

Figure 4-28. *Tarot cards*

If you must have text on your image, especially longer than a few words, DALL-E does better, though still imperfect.

Midjourney Troubleshooting

If you are satisfied with the style and composition but a detail is undesired, for example, hands are messed up:

1. Try Vary(Region), select the area you want to correct, and re-run the prompt. You can also just put "clean" as the prompt.

2. Try Vary(Strong) – it may result in similar images with no deficiencies.

3. Use multi-prompts and weights. You can exclude hands by adding "--no hands" to your prompt. Using "no" gives "hands" a negative weight of -0.5, while the default weight is 1. You can exclude hands "stronger" if you use explicit weights, for example, <prompt>::100 hands::-90. (With weights, what matters is their ratio.)

If the images are too complex and cluttered, add words like

1. Simple, minimal, primitive, basic, rudimentary

2. Clean, crisp lines

If the image is too simple or boring:

1. Add complex, intricate, complicated, or convoluted, vivid, vibrant, light, and shade

2. Bring in a time or place detail, for example, Middle Ages or Morocco

3. Raise the chaos and weird values up from their defaults

To improve the quality in v 5.2, use words like beautiful, gorgeous, and masterpiece.

These are some strong modifiers I frequently use to alter image styles. Sometimes, I use the entire set of three words in one prompt or select the individual words to include in a prompt:

- Real, realistic, photorealistic

- Stylized, symbolic, abstract

- Primitive, minimal, simple

- Surreal, psychedelic, whimsical

You will find a long list of strong modifiers in Appendix E.

Logos

Up to the latest improvements in v 6.0, Midjourney was not a tool for designing logos. However, with its better language understanding, it is becoming promising..

This ChatGPT description (of the LinkedIn Recruiter logo) comes close to producing a real logo.

Prompt: An icon or logo representing a magnifying glass, a common symbol for search or find functions. The design is simplistic and consists of a circular shape with a handle attached, representing the lens and handle of a traditional magnifying glass. The color is a solid blue, and there's a figure inside the circle that resembles a simplified human shape, suggesting a focus on people or profiles within the context of searching. --v 6.0 --style raw (see Figure 4-29)

Figure 4-29. *Search symbol, a logo*

Midjourney can be helpful to brainstorm ideas for new logos. In the following example, I asked Midjourney to generate AI logos.

Prompt: Simple large minimalistic creative unique 2-color logo meaning ai images, central text "AI" --v 6.0 --s 300 (see Figure 4-30)

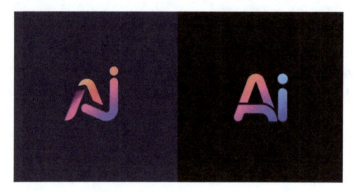

Figure 4-30. *"AI," a logo*

Summary

To summarize, this chapter covered the following advanced Midjourney techniques:

- Multi-prompts let you adjust image elements' prominence by assigning weights, balancing visuals in an image.

- Negative weights help exclude unwanted elements. However, excluded elements might still appear subtly.

- Upscaling in v 6.0 changes image styles, not just size, affecting clarity and adding creative elements.

- Styles and aesthetic parameters guide the image's look, using --style and --s parameters for different effects.

- Pan and Zoom expand the image beyond the initial frame, showing what's imagined outside the visible area.

- Controlling characters in v 6.0 improves character depiction precision by clearly structuring prompts.

- Text in v 6.0 has limitations; it may be repeated or misspelled.

- Troubleshooting offers solutions for common problems like undesired details or simplifying complex images.

- Midjourney is almost ready to create logos.

Experiment with these features for better results.

Let's move on to Chapter 5, which covers the differences and advantages of each version, as well as advanced techniques for creative image generation in Midjourney.

CHAPTER 5

Advanced Creative Techniques

This chapter explores advanced techniques in Midjourney, leveraging different versions and creative strategies for image generation. I highlight the contrasts between versions 5.2, 5.2R, and 6.0, emphasizing their unique strengths in response to specific prompts.

This chapter also introduces "bouncing," a method for combining the imaginative output of one version with the enhanced quality of another, and suggests using misspellings for unexpected results. It also covers a technique to blend the creativity of v 5.2 with the quality of v 6.0 using the Vary(Strong) command.

This section is essential for those experimenting with Midjourney's capabilities to produce diverse and unique images.

Midjourney Versions and Remixing Them

The latest Midjourney version is 6.0. When its Alpha version came out, following nine months of development, in December of 2023, the Midjourney community of users realized that it significantly differed from the previous version, 5.2. Its strong side is image stylizing. It also has a better understanding of longer prompts and natural language. But it does not have the vivid imagination of version 5.2.

© The Editor(s) (if applicable) and The Author(s),
under exclusive license to APress Media, LLC, part of Springer Nature 2024
I. Shamaeva, *Advanced Styles and Insights with Midjourney*,
https://doi.org/10.1007/979-8-8688-0336-9_5

Versions 5.2, 5.2R, and 6.0 have different algorithms/ways to render images. Nobody knows much about v 5.2R, but v 6.0 and v 5.2 were built on different datasets of images and associated words and phrases as well.

Here is a comparison of the versions using the following prompt.

Prompt: Sailor, old times. Different small pink crisp birds. Small birds build a nest in the sailor's hair, old times masterpiece, oil acrylic --no woman --v 6.0 (see Figure 5-1)

Figure 5-1. *Sailor and birds (v 6.0)*

Prompt: Sailor, old times. Different small pink crisp birds. Small birds build a nest in the sailor's hair, old times masterpiece, oil acrylic --no woman --v 5.2 (see Figure 5-2)

Figure 5-2. *Sailor and birds (v 5.2)*

Prompt: Sailor, old times. Different small pink crisp birds. Small birds build a nest in the sailor's hair, old times masterpiece, oil acrylic --no woman (v 5.2R) (see Figure 5-3)

Figure 5-3. *Sailor and birds (v 5.2R)*

With a given prompt, it may turn out that one of the versions or version combination would do very well:

- 6.0

- 5.2

- 5.2R

- A mix of the aforementioned, where you initially use a prompt in one version, then run Vary(Strong) on the resulting images with the prompt in a different version

Here are some examples of running different versions and combinations.

Prompt: A pretty white mouse masterpiece --v 6.0 (see Figure 5-4)

Figure 5-4. *Mouse (v 6.0)*

Prompt: A pretty white mouse masterpiece --v 5.2 (see Figure 5-5)

Figure 5-5. *Mouse (v 5.2)*

Prompt: A pretty white mouse masterpiece --v 5.2R (see Figure 5-6)

Figure 5-6. *Mouse (v 5.2R)*

Prompt: A pretty white mouse masterpiece (version 5.2 mixed with 6.0) (see Figure 5-7)

Figure 5-7. *Mouse (v 5.2 and v 6.0)*

Prompt: A pretty white mouse masterpiece (version 6.0 mixed with 5.2) (see Figure 5-8)

Figure 5-8. *Mouse (v 6.0 and v 5.2)*

Bouncing

Version 5.2 is imaginative. Version 6.0 would add quality and texture to the image created in v 5.2 if you run Vary(Strong) over the image, having changed the prompt to v 6.0.

"Bouncing" is my own term, and it amounts to the following:

1. Run a prompt in v 5.2

2. Using Vary(Strong), re-run the prompt in v 6.0

I recommend using short and vague or contradictory prompts to let v 5.2 shine.

Examples:

Prompt: Amazing nocturnes of light and shadows over a secluded lake ideal nostalgic atmospheric (see Figure 5-9)

Figure 5-9. *Nocturnes of light*

Prompt: Beautiful illuminated wild flowers (see Figure 5-10)

Figure 5-10. *Illuminated wild flowers*

Prompt: Flaring at Chevron refinery under investigation (see Figure 5-11)

Figure 5-11. _Chevron refinery_

Prompt: White egretorchid (I used a made-up word; see Figure 5-12)

Figure 5-12. _"Egretorchid"_

You can also try to "bounce" in the other direction, that is, 6 to 5.2, or bounce back and forth several times.

Using Vary(Region) to Combine the Imagination of v 5.2 and Quality of v 6.0

To create an image using v 5.2's imagination and v 6.0's quality, you can "bounce" – run the prompt in v 5.2 and re-run it over one of the resulting images in v 6.0. I have also come up with another technique that would keep the image close to the original while upgrading the aesthetics.

Create an image in 5.2, then use two or three Vary(Region) commands to select large areas, for example, the top half, and then the bottom half in the subsequent run while changing the version to 6.

Here is an example.

Prompt: A 2 by 2 character faces design sheet with different angles for a charming naive real-life creature named Gertrude, perfect --v 5.2 (see Figure 5-13)

Figure 5-13. *A grid in v 5.2*

I used the output from step 1 (Figure 5-13) and ran three Vary(Region) s over it, having changed the version to v 6.0. In other words, I selected large parts of the image (Figure 5-13) in Vary(Region) and re-ran with the prompt "a 2 by 2 character faces design sheet with different angles for a charming naive real-life creature named Gertrude, perfect --v 6.0."

This has kept the creature style while upgrading the aesthetics and congruence (see Figure 5-14)

Figure 5-14. *A grid in v 5.2/v 6.0*

Generally, I find v 5.2's creatures more attractive than v 6.0's. I am less satisfied with what v 6.0 alone has created for the prompt (see Figure 5-15).

Figure 5-15. *A grid in v 6.0*

The Power of Misspellings

If you misspell a word or use an imaginary word, Midjourney may guess the meaning and render the subject in unusual ways.

Prompt: Ovumflora sunnysidus

5.2/6 bounce (see Figure 5-16)

Figure 5-16. *Ovumflora sunnysidus*

Prompt: Brrkfst --v 6.0 --s 50 (see Figure 5-17)

Figure 5-17. Brrkfst

Prompt: Koalaroo full body Australian masterpiece (v 5.2R) (see Figure 5-18)

Figure 5-18. *"Koalaroo"*

Summary

This chapter covered versions, their combinations, and various advanced techniques for creative image generation in Midjourney:

- Experiment with different Midjourney versions (v 5.2, v 5.2R, and v 6.0) and their combinations to find the best fit for your artistic goals.

- Bouncing: Alternate between Midjourney versions (v 5.2 and v 6.0) to combine v 5.2's creativity with v 6.0's enhanced quality.

- Use misspelled prompts to prompt unique interpretations and surprise results.

The next chapter covers a topic of interest to many Midjourney users. How close can we come to creating a consistent character, varying their expressions, clothing, actions, and environment, and depicting them at different ages?

CHAPTER 6

Consistent Characters

A "consistent character" is subjective. A collection of images may portray the same person for some viewers and different for others. It is easier to create consistency if your character is stylized and has distinct features, such as black hair or red reading glasses.

Midjourney is not an ideal tool, but we like its aesthetics and can approach the task in several ways. In this chapter, I'll describe the following:

- Using image prompts and images as style references

- Creating "character sheets" using Pan and Zoom

- Using the new character reference parameter

Image Prompts and Images As Style References

I created a consistent character, a prehistoric boy and his family, back with Midjourney v 5.2, illustrating my friend Elena Jdanova's book *The Boy Who Tamed the Scorching Beast:: A Tale of Fire Domestication.*

I started off with an image of a boy created with the prompt: photo of a handsome, curious biracial tribal boy wearing a caveman outfit, prehistoric, old times, fairy tale character design, beautiful, watercolor oil pastel --v 5.2 (Figure 6-1).

© The Editor(s) (if applicable) and The Author(s),
under exclusive license to APress Media, LLC, part of Springer Nature 2024
I. Shamaeva, *Advanced Styles and Insights with Midjourney*,
https://doi.org/10.1007/979-8-8688-0336-9_6

Figure 6-1. *Prehistoric boy, initial image*

And then I ran prompts first with this image (Figure 6-1) with multiple image references that looked similar.

Example prompt: <URL of the image in Figure 6-1> watercolor photo of biracial tribal boy with gray ashes on his forehead from smoke, prehistoric, old times, fairy tale character design, beautiful, watercolor oil pastel --v 5.2 --q 2 --s 750 (Figure 6-2)

Figure 6-2. *Prehistoric boy, variation*

I continued with prompts like the following: <multiple image URLs> photo of a handsome curious biracial tribal boy full body in primitive handmade leather shoes in a cave eating berries, prehistoric, old times, fairy tale character design, beautiful, watercolor oil pastel --v 5.2 (Figure 6-3).

Figure 6-3. *Book cover image*

Prompt to create the boy's family members: Photo of a beautiful handsome biracial tribal family and grandma gathered around the fire in the cave, prehistoric, old times, fairy tale character design, beautiful, watercolor oil pastel --ar 16:9 --v 5.2 --q 2 --s 750 (Figure 6-4)

Figure 6-4. *Boy's family*

Here is another attempt to create a consistent character with v 6.0 (which is hard for a realistic style portrait) in different Midjourney sessions using prompts.

I created a woman's portrait to be used as the base. I used prompts with empty text, stressing the image usage, like the following: <URL of the woman's portrait> "" --style raw --sref <URL of the woman's portrait> --sw 1000 --iw 3 --v 6.0 (Figure 6-5).

It was difficult to incorporate any different details – like putting glasses on the woman – since Midjourney focused on processing images.

Figure 6-5. *Consistent character, a woman*

Character Sheets, Pan, and Zoom Out

Consistent characters are more likely to appear within one Midjourney run. I started with the first image and did a few zoom-outs and pans, using the following prompt while increasing the numbers X and Y (Figure 6-6).

Prompt: A <X> by <Y> turnaround sheet with many, many different views of a pretty stylized girl Lily oil acrylic --v 6.0

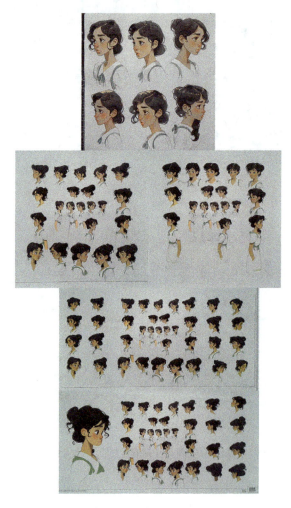

Figure 6-6. *Turnaround sheet with many views*

Character Reference, --cref

The new option, character references, is run with the syntax "--cref <image>" and optional parameter --cw varying from 0 to 100; 100 is the default. At 0, --cw copies the face only; at 100, all of the outfit as well. This latest addition does a fine job reproducing "the same" face. However, placing your hero in different environments and adding moods or actions may still be challenging.

The following is a series of portraits using the word "portrait" and previously produced images as --cref parameters (Figure 6-7).

Figure 6-7. *Results of "character reference"*

Summary

In this chapter, I have shared how I navigated the complexities of creating consistent characters using Midjourney. I used image prompts in a storytelling project to develop a cohesive look for a prehistoric family. I came close to generating consistent, realistic portraits of a woman. An option to create characters more consistently is to use character sheets in combination with Pan and Zoom Out. Finally, you can use the newest "character reference" function.

The next chapter discusses using AI tools, like ChatGPT and Google's Gemini, for writing prompts. You feed these tools examples of what you like, and they adapt, producing prompts in your preferred style.

CHAPTER 7

Use AI for Prompt Creation

Let us look at writing prompts using AI tools like ChatGPT and Google's Gemini, which can assist in generating wording and ideas for artistic themes. You can interact with these systems to refine prompts to your preference. The chapter also covers teaching ChatGPT your preferred prompt style by feeding it example prompts and then asking it to generate new ones, demonstrating AI's ability to learn and adapt to user preferences.

Write Prompts with ChatGPT and Gemini

ChatGPT and other AI systems can help you find the wording or terminology for your prompts. Whether you want to draw ancient history, classic cars, modern fashion, or use any particular artistic style, you can get lists of suggestions.

ChatGPT, Google's Gemini, and other AI systems can also create image prompts when you have a topic or idea and want a detailed prompt. You can have a dialog with the system and ask it to modify the prompt to your liking.

For example, I asked ChatGPT and Gemini to "write an AI image prompt for an outstanding black-and-white street photo" and rendered their output in Midjourney.

Prompt by ChatGPT: Imagine a sunlit, bustling city street framed in black and white. At the center, a cyclist navigates through a crowd of pedestrians, their motion blurred slightly to convey movement. Around them, the architecture spans from quaint shops to towering skyscrapers, each detail crisp under the harsh daylight. Shadows cast by trees and buildings create patterns on the pavement, adding depth and texture. --v 6.0 --style raw (Figure 7-1)

Figure 7-1. *City street in black and white (ChatGPT prompt)*

With the Gemini-generated prompt, I chose to use a high --s value (Figure 7-2):

Prompt: A high-contrast black and white street photograph bathed in warm afternoon sunlight. A lone figure, silhouetted against a bustling cityscape, walks purposefully down a rain-slicked cobblestone street lined with vintage lampposts casting long shadows. Capture the fleeting moment with a shallow depth of field, blurring the background activity and emphasizing the solitary figure's quiet determination. --v 6.0 --s 900

Figure 7-2. *Black and white street photograph (Gemini prompt)*

Teach ChatGPT with Your Prompts

Artificial Intelligence learns from examples. Once you have a set of prompts you like, you can feed it to ChatGPT and tell it to understand the style, then produce other prompts. You would be more successful if your prompts were similar, but I fed ChatGPT a set of diverse prompts, and its output prompts are in a style that mainly creates unique, exciting images.

Step 1. I collected a list of my prompts and stripped it of styles and versions:

- A dragon with eyes and tail, patchwork Maori

- A dressed insect

- A futuristic city skyline with neon lights and flying cars, a cyberpunk theme, digital neon oil painting

- A garden of bioluminescent flowers under a full moon, fantasy, neon watercolors with dark contrasts

- A park with miniature fantasy castles, fairies flying around, in an enchanted pastel

- A portrait in metal and leather, a masterpiece

103

- A road in the hills, iridescent holographic fantasy acrylic oil ink

- A severe argument between two insects in acrylic

- A theorem of Pythagoras

- A town made of silver threads, tiny red bubbles, holiday pine needles, perfect greeting card

- A vintage friendly art New Year card, text "Happy New Year!" on the card

- A Vogue woman holding a white goose stylized

- An abstract Braille flower

- An owl Jeff Soto style

- An unusual house with various doors stands on a hill. The doors are made of wood and metal. The hill is covered with snow. The house is painted by hand. A little cat walks nearby. Acrylic ink

- Angles with wigns

- Animals closeup, stippling style

- Axolotl full body is made of thin paper, dressed as a princess, chiaroscuro

- Barking trees, rain and wind, crayon acrylic pastel

- Bright, vivid winter celebration, wet-on-wet oil

- Bright woolly woven winter wonder land crayon charcoal

- Brushed hammered bronze and metal creatures, ideal

- Byzantine empress in her court, opulent palace, rich mosaic with intricate patterns and jewel tones

- Dancing bluebells and flowers, rain and wind, native art::100 woman::-80

- Delicate inspiring winter wonder, alcohol ink, frozen air, glossy owl contours

- Double shade reflections of wonders

- Drunken sailor, stripes of paper glued onto wood exquisite portrait, 1800s

- Egyptian pyramids, sun-drenched desert, hieroglyphic style with gold and lapis lazuli accents

- Electrostatic ink wash windy windy winter road

- Elegant, delicate clockwork animals melting timepieces, vibrant oil pastels

- Fairy tale Christmas, oil acrylic ink

- Five different animals stand together. The first animal is a rat. The rat is black and wearing glasses. The second animal is a hippo. The hippo is warmly dressed. The third animal is a cow. The cow wears a purple belt. The fourth animal is a possum. The possum is wearing overalls. The fifth animal is a wise owl. The owl has blue eyes. The snow is light

- Forget-me-not memory game

- Ghostly pirate ship sailing through the stars, cosmic ocean, glow-in-the-dark acrylics

- Glitter showers oil acrylic ink

- Half-moon, half-sun face fauvism

- He froig is full of himself

- Hooded friendly human aliens live in a woven basket universe

- If Pixar made the Harry Potter series

- In non-Euclid geometry, landscapes are connected to towns by tubes

- Kids playing hide and seek in a giant, ancient tree with doorways leading to magical realms

- Knights jousting on mechanical horses, medieval steampunk fair, rustic oil painting with iron-like textures

- Little rockets are flying to vivid non-Euclid geometry seamless planets

- Lost city of Atlantis rising from the ocean, sunken ruins, deep blue, and sea green encaustic wax

- Lush gardens on the moon fantasy, acrylic pastel ink painting, binary backdrop, insane colors

- Majestic dragons soaring over the Great Wall of China, sunrise hues, traditional Chinese brushwork

- Maori art

- My portrait with possums on a candid wall

- Mystic shaman summoning spirit animals in a neon jungle, psychedelic, fluorescent acrylics

- Mystical forest made of crystal and gemstone, ethereal creatures, luminous acrylic with glitter highlights

- Old English folk tale vignettes, ideal

- Old English town, cobbled streets, lit shop windows, by Marc Chagall
- Orchestra of mythical creatures playing in an ancient amphitheater, moonlit night, watercolor with luminescent ink
- Possum and peas
- Queen of the forest with her animal court, enchanted woods, rich tapestry style with natural dyes
- Quiet evening, shadow art
- Retro 1950s diner on Mars, classic cars and robots, pop art style with bold colors and sharp contrasts
- Space pirates looting a cosmic train, asteroid belt, gritty charcoal with starlight highlights
- Starry swirly lines backdrop
- Tall blue aliens with friendly yellow tiny creatures
- Tall green aliens meet friendly pink, tiny fluffy creatures
- The fantastic black belt in Martian arts, Korean African
- The inflated orchestrator closeup
- The quiet, magical cool volcano of dots
- The ruler of centimeters acrylic oil pastel ink
- The silent eggheads stylized
- The social nerds MENSA club pencil drawing
- The world is my white symbolic oyster, oil acrylic watercolor
- There is a house in the mouse
- This is a way to achieve a close likeness

- Time-traveling detectives in Victorian London, foggy streets, monochrome graphite with subtle color pops

- Trader Joe's flyers, often referred to as the "Fearless Flyer," have a distinctive style that's best described as a combination of old-fashioned newsletter and modern catalog. A vintage, hand-drawn look, reminiscent of classic newspapers and advertising flyers, characterizes the style. This aesthetic is complemented by the text's playful and witty tone, making the flyers both visually unique and entertaining to read

- The train station where trains travel through time, historic and futuristic, sepia and neon-toned mixed media

- Two-faced Janus masterpiece

- Underwater jazz club, octopus band, coral stage, bioluminescent audience, watercolor glow

- Uneven, non-glossy, unique, unpolished, unrefined, unsmooth, untamed animal

- Unique holiday customs from various cultures, photorealistic

- Various crumpled paper trees with berries, fairy tale

- Vibrant glamorous models walk on a catwalk, the roaring 20s, cartoon with crayon

- Victorian-era robots at a garden tea party, sepia-toned watercolor with pencil details

- Vintage, hand-drawn "Trader Joes" flyer, healthy, unique, and gourmet items, text "Trader Joes" on top of the flyer

- Vivid, colorful, airy lace filigree winter folk landscape

- Weightless orange people

- White black red NYC model walk

Step 2. I gave the list to ChatGPT and asked it to analyze the style:

> **ChatGPT**
>
> The style of these prompts showcases a blend of artistic techniques, themes, and settings. They range from the whimsical and surreal, like animals dressed in human attire and bioluminescent gardens, to the fantastical and mythological, with dragons and magical forests. The descriptions are vivid and specific, designed to evoke detailed images that blend the natural with the supernatural or the modern with the historical.
>
> The prompts also play with artistic styles, referencing various materials and mediums such as acrylic, pastel, oil, watercolor, and stippling. Some prompts suggest a 3D aspect, like the "town made of silver threads," while others are more abstract, like the "abstract Braille flower."
>
> Overall, these prompts are crafted to generate images that are not just visually striking but also rich in storytelling, each creating a unique world or scenario that could evoke curiosity and engagement. They seem tailored for an audience that appreciates art, creativity, and the unexpected twists in visual representation.

Step 3. I asked ChatGPT to create 20 prompts in the style (no other directions). Result – these are new prompt starters:

- A baker's secret midnight feast, with pastries shaped like the moon's phases, captured in silvery charcoal

- A hidden garden where the flowers change colors with the sound of a violin, painted in shifting watercolors

- A tailor's shop where the clothes design themselves, swirling with patterns that tell stories in vibrant silk threads, stylized

- A quiet library where the characters pop out of the books and roam the aisles, sketched in the magical realism style

- A cobblestone street that flows like a river during the rain, pedestrians hopping on stones in glistening oil paint

- A secret café where each cup of coffee reveals your dreams in its steam, illustrated in misty pastels

- A playground at night where the swings sway gently on their own under a starry sky in glow-in-the-dark acrylic

- An antique clock shop where time moves backward, the hands dancing counterclockwise in a surrealistic graphite style

- A flower stall where each bouquet arranges itself based on the buyer's aura, in luminescent inks

- A barber's where each snip of hair plays a note, creating a symphony with each haircut, depicted in musical watercolor notes

- A bustling kitchen where the utensils are alive, stirring and chopping rhythmically in animated oil pastels

- A cozy attic where the dust motes tell ancient stories, illuminated by shafts of light in golden sepia tones

- A street where the shadows play tag with the pedestrians, cast in dynamic charcoal

- A laundromat where the washing machines spin stories instead of clothes, bubbles painted in iridescent acrylic

- A rainy bus stop where each raindrop whispers a different piece of poetry, sketched in melancholic blues

- It is a winter's day where each snowflake is a tiny ice sculpture, a frozen gallery on streets, in crystalline watercolors

- An elevator that takes you to forgotten floors of your memories, doors opening to past scenes in nostalgic pastels

- A mirror in a boutique that reflects not your image but your potential self in multifaceted oil strokes

- A bridge that arches over a river of time, people crossing back into memories in sepia-toned vignettes

- It is a cozy evening where the shadows of the furniture, cast in soft amber acrylics, tell their tales of the day

Ten historical prompts in the style. Result:

- A Renaissance artist's studio, with unfinished inventions and paintings that come to life, sketched in the flickering light of oil lamps, using da Vinci's sfumato technique

- Rich lapis lazuli and gold leaf capture a Pharaoh's court during a feast, with a hieroglyphic fresco animating the celebration

- A medieval scriptorium, where monks illuminate manuscripts with ink that glows with their thoughts in detailed gothic miniature style

- A 1920s jazz club where the music's rhythm visibly swirls around the dancers illustrated with Art Deco flair and bold, brassy colors

- A Victorian séance room with partially visible ghostly figures rendered in a spectral mix of watercolor and gaslight glow

- A 17th-century pirate ship where the sails billow with the sea's whispered secrets in stormy charcoal and saltwash

- A speakeasy during Prohibition, where the clink of glasses reveals hidden messages captured in hushed sepia tones and secret ink

- A Silk Road bazaar at its zenith, where each tapestry weaves the story of its journey in a tapestry of vibrant dyes and textures

- An ancient Greek amphitheater during a play, where the actors' shadows play out the story behind the script in sunbaked terracotta hues

- A roaring 1940s newsroom on election night, where the ink on the papers shifts with the changing headlines in dynamic grayscale and flashes of victory red

Ten prompts with imaginary creatures. Result:

- A garden where each flower blooms into a tiny dragon with butterfly wings, their scales shimmering in the sunlight, depicted in jewel-toned watercolors

- A nocturnal forest where the trees are gentle giants with eyes that watch over wandering travelers, painted in moonlit hues and silver leaf

- An underground cave where the stalactites are actually sleeping bat-cats, their wings folded around them, in luminescent mineral paints

- A bustling city square where invisible creatures leave paw prints in the snow, each print a different color, illustrated in sparkling frosty pastels

- A coral reef where each anemone is home to sea sprites, their delicate forms barely visible among the fronds in translucent watercolor layers

- A mountaintop where the wind is made visible by the swirling air spirits, their forms twisting in the currents, captured in whirling charcoal strokes

- A desert oasis where mirage beasts offer visions of water to travelers, their forms shimmering in heatwave distortions in a mirage of iridescent inks

- A twilight meadow where each firefly is a tiny lantern bird, their glowing beaks leading the way to dreamland in neon acrylics

- An ancient library where the books are guarded by literate lions with glasses perched on their noses, illustrated in warm sepia tones and leather-bound textures

- A frozen tundra where the snowmen come to life at night, dancing under the auroras with their broomstick arms in a dance of glow-in-the-dark watercolors

For most of these AI-generated prompts, results are satisfying; sometimes, it makes sense to alter the prompt with a style or keywords to improve the output.

Summary

This chapter showed how to guide AI in generating the prompts you want. We learned the importance of clear instructions and examples to shape the AI's output. The next chapter is about tools that can provide you with a description of a given image.

CHAPTER 8

Image-to-Text Tools

If you run across an image you like, you can try to draw something similar by describing it first with a dedicated tool and then using the description as a prompt. Do not expect to get an exact copy with any tools, but you may enjoy their interpretation of the subject and style.

Midjourney's /describe

Midjourney has a /describe function. On Discord, you can give it an image, and it will provide four alternative prompts at a time, which you can render. The generated prompts may be good inspiration, and with the recently improved /describe, sometimes produce images close to the original.

As an example, here is an image that I wanted to describe (Figure 8-1).

© The Editor(s) (if applicable) and The Author(s),
under exclusive license to APress Media, LLC, part of Springer Nature 2024
I. Shamaeva, *Advanced Styles and Insights with Midjourney*,
https://doi.org/10.1007/979-8-8688-0336-9_8

Figure 8-1. *A bird, an image to describe*

Here is what the /describe function has produced, rendered in Midjourney – great images, but different from the original (Figure 8-2):

1. A colorful painting of a bird with a heart for the water, in the style of whimsical melancholy, black paintings, melting, mark briscoe, mandy disher, joyful celebration of nature, somber mood

2. An artist painted an intricate painting of a bird with a crow, a flower and a heart, in the style of water drops, expressionist angst, henri le sidaner, aaron jasinski, cheerful colors, andrea kowch, emotive expressionism

3. A large bird is represented in this painting, in the style of whimsical melancholy, water drops, melting pots, humor meets heart, playfully dark, tupinipunk, colorful gardens

4. Colorful painting with a bird in the middle of
    a flower patch, in the style of water drops, dark
    whimsy, emotional storytelling, humor meets heart,
    moche art, textural landscapes, pigeoncore

Figure 8-2. *Birds described in Midjourney*

In Midjourney's /describe output text, you may see words ending in
-core, -punk, or -wave like "applecore" and "dieselpunk." They do not have
a special Midjourney meaning beyond the part preceding -punk, etc. A
collection of those is presented in Appendix D.

ChatGPT Image Describe

If you want to create something similar to the image you have, ChatGPT (the paid version) will provide you with a long, succinct prompt. Microsoft Copilot can provide image descriptions as well.

When I asked to describe the image (Figure 8-1), ChatGPT produced the following paragraph, and I gave it to Midjourney (Figure 8-3):

Prompt: Create an image of a whimsical, surreal landscape at night. The scene is filled with a variety of stylized, colorful flowers and plants, some with unique patterns and others glowing as if lit from within. At the center, there is a large, fantastical bird with a patterned body standing beside a circular pond that reflects the night sky. The bird has a prominent heart shape on its chest and an oversized beak. Its feathers are adorned with intricate designs featuring leaves, flowers, and abstract shapes. Surrounding the bird and pond are celestial objects like stars, a crescent moon, and planets, stylized with vibrant colors and textures that give a dreamy, magical atmosphere. The overall color palette is rich and dark, with highlights of bright colors to accentuate the mystical flora and fauna. --v 6.0 --s 200 --c 10

Figure 8-3. *Bird described in ChatGPT*

Gemini Image Describe

You can also ask for an image description (Figure 8-1) of Google Gemini by uploading an image and telling it to describe it. Gemini tends to see more realism in images.

Here is a typical reply, which I have shortened before running as a prompt in Midjourney.

"The image you sent me is a colorful painting of a bird with a heart on its chest. The bird is standing in a pond, surrounded by water lilies and other aquatic plants. The background is a lush green forest. The overall impression of the painting is one of peace and tranquility."

Here are some additional details about the painting:

- The bird is a blue jay, with bright blue feathers on its back and wings. Its chest is white, with a large red heart in the center.

- The water lilies in the pond are pink and white. There are also some green cattails growing in the background.

- The forest in the background is green and leafy. There are a few birds flying in the sky."

Figure 8-4. *Bird described in Gemini*

Midjourney prompt: The image you sent me is a colorful painting of a bird with a heart on its chest. The bird is standing in a pond, surrounded by water lilies and other aquatic plants. The background is a lush green forest. The overall impression of the painting is one of peace and tranquility. The bird is a blue jay, with bright blue feathers on its back and wings. Its chest is white, with a large red heart in the center. The water lilies in the pond are pink and white. There are also some green cattails growing in the background. The forest in the background is green and leafy. There are a few birds flying in the sky. --v 6.0 --s 50.

Summary

This chapter highlighted tools for converting images into text prompts for creative use in Midjourney:

- Midjourney's /describe: Generates alternative prompts from images, with some closely replicating the original scene, while others offering different, creative inspirations

- ChatGPT Plus Image Describe: Provides detailed prompts based on images to replicate the original scene in Midjourney

- Google Image Gemini Describe: Delivers realistic image descriptions, focusing on detail and impression, which is helpful for creating accurate prompts in Midjourney

These tools offer varied approaches for translating visual content into descriptive prompts, facilitating different levels of fidelity and creativity in image recreation.

You cannot learn the art of AI images by only reading even the best books or watching video tutorials. Hands-on practice must accompany the learning. Get to know Midjourney by directly interacting with it and using diverse prompts.

In the next chapter, I will provide several exercises, which will help you to explore particular techniques in Midjourney.

CHAPTER 9

Midjourney Challenges (Exercises) for You

This chapter offers some exercises designed to help you to explore various Midjourney's capabilities hands-on.

Challenge #1: Textures

Combine two or more textures in a drawing. The more, the merrier! Make your textures stand out. Appendix B has a list of textures. Add lights and shadows as you please to enhance the outcome.

Attached are images for prompts (Figure 9-1):

- Meshed dotted striped swirled apple tree --v 6.0

- Velvety holographic apple tree shadow --v 6.0

- Embossed waxy marbled apple tree --v 6.0

- Embossed waxy apple tree shadows --v 6.0

© The Editor(s) (if applicable) and The Author(s),
under exclusive license to APress Media, LLC, part of Springer Nature 2024
I. Shamaeva, *Advanced Styles and Insights with Midjourney*,
https://doi.org/10.1007/979-8-8688-0336-9_9

Figure 9-1. *Apple trees in textures*

Challenge #2: Pairs of Colors

Create images using pairs of colors. See Appendix F for color suggestions.

Example 1: Mint Green and Raspberry vintage imaginary aircraft (v 5.2/6.0 bounce) (Figure 9-2)

The first image is produced in v 5.2, then bounced to v 6.0 using Vary(Strong). For more information on bouncing, refer to Chapter 5.

Figure 9-2. *Mint Green and Raspberry*

Example 2: A bug made of metal and copper wire, dark yellow and teal, macro, smooth, reflective --v 6.0 --s 450 (Figure 9-3)

Figure 9-3. *Dark yellow and teal*

Example 3: Teal and Coral Pink colored exquisite dessert flyer --v 6.0 --s 600 (Figure 9-4)

Figure 9-4. *Teal and Coral Pink*

Challenge #3: Structured Prompts

1. Start with landscape, cityscape, house, portrait, or room.

2. Add time and/or place, for example, the roaring 1920s or Vienna.

3. Add qualities (adjectives) like mesmerizing, seamless, crooked, or stretched.

4. Define the media, like acrylic impasto or spray painting.

5. Add the mood, for example, nostalgic, delightful, or gloomy.

6. Add the backdrop, for example, full moon backdrop.

Examples:

Prompt: 1960s San Francisco street, psychedelic, oil painting, nostalgic mood, Golden Gate Bridge backdrop --s 50 --v 6.0 (Figure 9-5)

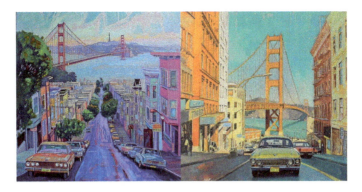

Figure 9-5. *Golden Gate Bridge backdrop*

Prompt: Caribbean pirate captain, adventurous, watercolor ink, nautical theme, naive fairy tale --c 15 (Figure 9-6)

Figure 9-6. *Caribbean pirate captain*

Other example prompts:

- Underwater coral reef, vibrant, watercolor, tranquil mood, sunbeam piercing water backdrop.

- 1960s San Francisco street, psychedelic, oil painting, nostalgic mood, Golden Gate Bridge backdrop.

- Renaissance Florence square, historical, tempera, reflective mood, Duomo view backdrop.

- Amazon rainforest, lush, gouache, mysterious mood, exotic wildlife backdrop.

- Viking village, rustic, woodcut print, resilient mood, northern lights backdrop.

- Medieval Japanese garden, peaceful, Sumi-e ink, contemplative mood, cherry blossom backdrop.

- Steampunk London alley, intricate, graphite pencil, curious mood, foggy Thames backdrop.

- Moon colony, futuristic, digital 3D, awe mood, Earthrise backdrop.

- 1950s American diner, nostalgic, pastel chalk, cheerful mood, classic car backdrop.

- Ancient Egyptian marketplace, bustling, papyrus style, historic mood, pyramids backdrop.

- Alien planet landscape, surreal, neon airbrush, wonder mood, two suns backdrop.

- Himalayan monastery, serene, thangka painting, spiritual mood, snowy peaks backdrop.

- Jazz Age New Orleans, lively, charcoal, musical mood, Mississippi River backdrop.

- Cyberpunk Tokyo intersection, neon-lit, digital vector, energetic mood, skyscraper backdrop.

- Arctic research base, isolated, minimalist watercolor, introspective mood, aurora borealis backdrop.

- Venetian carnival, mysterious, oil pastel, festive mood, Grand Canal backdrop.

- Appalachian trail, autumn, colored pencil, peaceful mood, mountain range backdrop.

- 1930s Shanghai street, historical, ink wash, dynamic mood, Art Deco architecture backdrop.

- Mars rover landing site, stark, acrylic pour, pioneering mood, red Martian soil backdrop.

- Australian Outback, rugged, dot painting, adventurous mood, Uluru backdrop.

- 18th century Paris salon, elegant, Rococo style, cultural mood, Versailles backdrop.

- Caribbean pirate ship, adventurous, watercolor, thrilling mood, tropical island backdrop.

- Medieval European village, quaint, tempera, peaceful mood, castle backdrop.

- Silicon Valley startup office, modern, digital graphic, innovative mood, tech campus backdrop.

- Ancient Greek amphitheater, historic, charcoal sketch, dramatic mood, Acropolis backdrop.

- 1980s Miami beachfront, vibrant, pastel oil, lively mood, Art Deco buildings backdrop.

- Deep space nebula, cosmic, spray paint, mystical mood, star cluster backdrop.

- Mongolian steppe, vast, traditional felt art, nomadic mood, yurt village backdrop.

- Prehistoric cave, primitive, charcoal, ochre, ancestral mood, cave painting backdrop.

- Renaissance scholar, thoughtful, oil on canvas, inspired by Leonardo da Vinci.

- 1920s flapper girl, glamorous, charcoal and pastel, Art Deco influence.

- Viking warrior, fierce, woodcut style, Northern European art traditions.

- Ancient Egyptian queen, regal, papyrus-like texture, hieroglyphic elements.

- Samurai warrior, stoic, Japanese ink wash, traditional calligraphy style.

- Steampunk inventor, eccentric, graphite pencil, Victorian-era detailing.

- Futuristic astronaut, visionary, digital 3D art, space-age aesthetics.

- 1950s rockabilly musician, cool, acrylic pop art, retro Americana vibes.

- Medieval knight, noble, tempera on wood, Gothic art style.

- Jazz Age musician, soulful, watercolor, New Orleans jazz culture.

- Cyberpunk hacker, edgy, neon digital vector, high-tech urban feel.

- Arctic explorer, resilient, minimalist watercolor, polar environment.

- Venetian masquerade attendee, mysterious, oil pastel, Baroque richness.

- Appalachian hiker, rugged, colored pencil, natural wilderness.

- 1930s Shanghai socialite, elegant, ink wash, Art Deco Shanghai style.

- Mars colonist, pioneering, acrylic pour, Martian landscape integration.

- Australian Aboriginal elder, wise, dot painting technique, indigenous art.

- 18th-century French aristocrat, refined, Rococo style, Versailles-inspired.

- Caribbean pirate captain, adventurous, watercolor, nautical theme.

- Medieval European farmer, humble, tempera and gold leaf, folk style.

- Silicon Valley tech entrepreneur, innovative, digital graphic, modern tech environment.

- Ancient Greek philosopher, contemplative, charcoal sketch, classical Greek art.

- 1980s Miami detective, stylish, pastel oil, neon-lit cityscape.

- Deep space explorer, cosmic, spray paint, interstellar backdrop.

- Mongolian horseman, nomadic, traditional felt art, steppe scenery.

- Prehistoric tribal leader, primal, charcoal, ochre, cave painting style.

- Baroque composer, artistic, oil on canvas, European Baroque era.

- Victorian scientist, inquisitive, detailed pen and ink, scientific instruments.

- Harlem Renaissance poet, expressive, Harlem-inspired watercolor, jazz elements.

- Ancient Roman senator, dignified, fresco style, Roman architecture.

Challenge #4: Glass

Create paintings using "glass" as your media.

Glass can have these qualities: glittering, stained, shimmering, frosted, clear, translucent, reflective, sparkling, Murano, tempered, smoky, etched, beveled, opaque, iridescent, polished, tinted, blown, crystalline, fluted, textured, seeded, lead, laminated.

Example image prompts rendered (Figure 9-7):

- A vivid crushed glass painting of a mouse --v 6.0

- A depiction of the Grand Canyon at sunset, with layers of crushed glass in reds, oranges, and purples conveying the depth and majesty of the landscape --v 5.2 --s 50

- A crushed glass tornado, Midwest (v 5.2R) (I used Vary(Region) to access v 5.2R. Refer to Chapter 1 for more information on v 5.2R)

Figure 9-7. *Glass images*

Here are some sample crushed glass prompts – or prompt starters to make your own:

- A bustling New York street, taxis and crowds captured in multicolored crushed glass, reflecting the city's vibrant energy.

- An intricate Moroccan mosaic, using only crushed glass to create complex patterns and designs that mirror traditional tile art.

- The Northern Lights, with crushed glass in greens, blues, and purples, create a shimmering effect that mimics this natural phenomenon.

- A detailed world map showcases global diversity, with each country represented by different shades and textures of crushed glass.

- A dynamic depiction of a jazz band, with musicians and instruments formed from crushed glass, captures the music's movement and rhythm.

- An ancient Egyptian pharaoh's portrait uses gold and blue crushed glass to reflect the opulence and mystery of that era.

- A serene Japanese Zen garden, with raked patterns in crushed glass representing sand and larger glass pieces as rocks, inviting contemplation.

- A vibrant coral reef scene, with crushed glass in a multitude of colors to represent the diverse marine life and corals.

- A bustling café scene in Paris, with patrons and street views captured in crushed glass, reflecting the city's romantic atmosphere.

- An African savannah at dusk, with wildlife silhouettes in crushed glass against a backdrop of a glass mosaic sunset.

- A Venetian canal, with the reflections of buildings and gondolas in the water, was created using various tones of crushed blue and green glass.

- A detailed rendering of the Milky Way galaxy, using crushed glass to capture the vastness and beauty of space.

- A scene from a bustling Indian festival, with crushed glass representing the explosion of colors, people, and activities.

- An abstract representation of a city's heartbeat, using crushed glass in a spectrum of colors to convey the energy and pulse of urban life.

Challenge #5: Fill the Space

Start by creating a space such as an empty room. Use Vary(Region) to select parts of the image and place different objects in the space by modifying the prompt.

Here is a basic example (Figure 9-8):

1. Prompt: Light and bright empty room --v 5.2

2. Vary(Region) with

   – Classic car

   – Striped cats

   – Christmas tree

   – Monkey hanging

Figure 9-8. *An empty room filled with various subjects*

Challenge #6: Design a Character Sheet

You aim to present your character in an image in several ways, like different poses or facial expressions. If you are ambitious, you can try to show someone's age progression. Your subject can be a person, an animal, or any creature.

Prompts may say something like "a character model sheet," or "360-degree views of," or perhaps "a day in the life of…."

In the following, you will find this:

Prompt: Character model sheet of a grandma mouse --v 5.2 (Figure 9-9)

Figure 9-9. *Grandma mouse character*

Prompt: A turnaround sheet with five views of Professor X in glasses oil acrylic --v 5.2 (Figure 9-10)

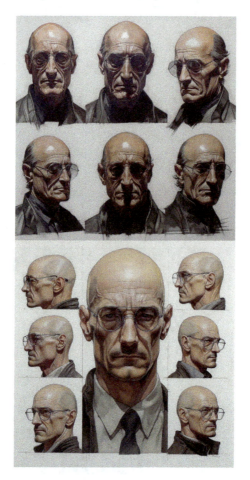

Figure 9-10. *Professor X character*

Challenge #7: Explore --style raw

In my experience, "style raw" produces more satisfactory results in
Midjourney v 6.0 than the default style. I like its aesthetics better. This
challenge is to re-run some of your prompts in v 6.0 --style raw.

Examples show "--style raw" on the left and the default style on the right.

Example 1 (Figure 9-11)

Left: The Lavender Lynxes of Lilac Ledge --v 6.0 --style raw

Right: The Lavender Lynxes of Lilac Ledge --v 6.0

Figure 9-11. *Lavender Lynxes*

Example 2 (Figure 9-12)

Left: An eccentric librarian is sitting alone at a café table, a book in one hand and a half-empty coffee cup in the other, lost in a moment of peace. stylized, bold and simple colors ink drawing, clean lines. 1960s --v 6.0 --style raw

Right: Prompt: An eccentric librarian is sitting alone at a café table, a book in one hand and a half-empty coffee cup in the other, lost in a moment of peace. stylized bold and simple colors ink drawing, clean lines. 1960s --v 6.0

Figure 9-12. *Librarian at a café table*

Example 3 (Figure 9-13)

Left: Imaginary fairy tale scene, awesome amazing unique elegant acrylic relief --v 6.0 --style raw

Right: Imaginary fairy tale scene, awesome amazing unique elegant acrylic relief --v 6.0

Figure 9-13. *Fairy tale relief*

Summary

In this chapter, I presented some exercises for you to play with different Midjourney techniques. In the final chapter, I want to share some of my Midjourney images and prompts.

CHAPTER 10

Conclusion and Sample Images with Prompts

This book has explored how to craft creative prompts to produce unique and captivating images. It provides examples that are both detailed and straightforward, merging the real with the fantastical. You've learned how to define versions, styles, and settings to precisely steer AI-driven image creation. The images showcased range from landscapes and animals to abstract concepts. The book introduces innovative Midjourney techniques, enabling you to leverage the strengths of its various versions. You've also discovered how to employ a mix of strategies, from image prompts to the "Vary" function, to diversify output styles.

At the end of the book, I want to share some of my latest images with you. Note: v 5.2R and 5.2/6.0 bounce are specific techniques I've discussed in Chapters 1 and 5, respectively, and not the actual parameters you would enter in the prompt.

© The Editor(s) (if applicable) and The Author(s),
under exclusive license to APress Media, LLC, part of Springer Nature 2024
I. Shamaeva, *Advanced Styles and Insights with Midjourney*,
https://doi.org/10.1007/979-8-8688-0336-9_10

Samples of My Prompts and Images

Prompt: The cat is reading sitting in a comfortable chair. Two small pretty ladies are sitting at his feet --v 6.0 --style raw (Figure 10-1).

Figure 10-1. *Reading cat*

Prompt: Wet origami paper gold cement folk tale folk art --v 6.0 --s 300 (Figure 10-2)

Figure 10-2. *Golden origami*

Prompt: Unfolding and blooming lotus, alchemy --v 6.0 --s 500 (Figure 10-3)

Figure 10-3. *Lotus*

Prompt: 1950s car-clock (v 5.2R) (Figure 10-4)

Figure 10-4. *Car-clock*

Prompt: A mild earthquake in my kitchen, whimsical --v 6.0 (Figure 10-5)

Figure 10-5. *Kitchen earthquake*

Prompt: Abstract path, gorgeous --v 6.0 --style raw --s 400 (Figure 10-6)

Figure 10-6. *Path*

Prompt: A city where buildings mimic chess pieces, pawns as homes and kings as skyscrapers, with streets as chessboard squares. Whimsical (5.2/6.0 bounce) (Figure 10-7)

Figure 10-7. Chess city

Prompt: Popcorn Cloud Machine: A whimsical machine on a hilltop, churning out clouds --v 6.0 --s 200 (Figure 10-8)

Figure 10-8. *Popcorn Cloud Machine*

Prompt: Dandelion Clock Tower: A tower with a clock face made from a giant dandelion, seeds ready to disperse with the wind, oil on canvas (5.2R) (Figure 10-9)

Figure 10-9. *Dandelion Clock Tower*

Prompt: Imaginary Italian fairy tale coast village, unique elegant acrylic relief --v 6.0 --s 300 (Figure 10-10)

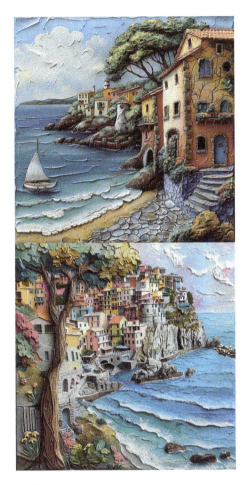

Figure 10-10. *Italian coast village*

Prompt: Monty Python --v 6.0 (Figure 10-11)

Figure 10-11. *Monty Python*

Prompt: A magical pirate ship trapped in a wave of water, acrylic impasto masterpiece --v 5.2 (Figure 10-12)

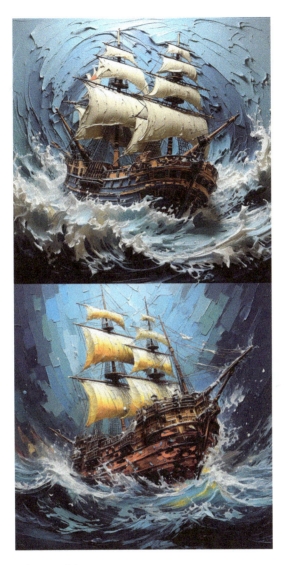

Figure 10-12. *Pirate ship*

That's a Wrap

Thanks for reading the book. Now, put these techniques to work and start creating your own standout visuals!

APPENDIX A

Styles and Descriptions

Use the following descriptions along with the style names as part of your prompts to render them in each style.

Style Names	Description
Ancient Egypt Papyrus	A detailed reproduction of an ancient Egyptian scroll, complete with hieroglyphics and traditional imagery.
Ancient Egyptian Art	A statue of an Egyptian pharaoh, sculpted with precision and adorned with hieroglyphs.
Animal Art	A vibrant painting of a jungle scene, featuring a variety of animals in a lush, detailed setting.
Anime	A dynamic illustration of an anime character in action, with exaggerated expressions and vibrant colors.
Aquatint Print	An aquatint etching of a moody landscape, using subtle gradations to create depth and atmosphere.
Architectural Art	A detailed pen and ink drawing of an iconic building, with precise lines and architectural details.
Architectural Photography	A striking photo of a modern skyscraper, capturing its geometric forms and the interplay of light and shadow.

(continued)

© The Editor(s) (if applicable) and The Author(s),
under exclusive license to APress Media, LLC, part of Springer Nature 2024
I. Shamaeva, *Advanced Styles and Insights with Midjourney*,
https://doi.org/10.1007/979-8-8688-0336-9

Style Names	Description
Art Deco	A poster design featuring bold geometric shapes, sharp lines, and a classic art deco color scheme.
Art Nouveau	An illustration with flowing, organic lines and stylized natural elements, embodying the elegance of Art Nouveau.
Arte Povera	An installation made from everyday materials, challenging the traditional concepts of art with its simplicity and rawness.
Asian Art	A delicate ink painting of a cherry blossom branch, showcasing the beauty and simplicity of traditional Asian aesthetics.
Assemblage Art	A three-dimensional collage created from found objects, each piece contributing to a cohesive narrative.
Augmented Reality	An interactive art piece that combines digital imagery with the real world when viewed through an AR app.
Autochrome	A photograph replicating the early color photography process, with soft, dreamlike colors.
Automatism	A drawing created without conscious thought, allowing the subconscious to direct the movement of the hand.
Aztec Carving	A stone sculpture inspired by Aztec mythology, intricately carved with gods and symbols.
Babylonian Art	A clay tablet inscribed with cuneiform script, depicting a scene from ancient Mesopotamian mythology.
Balance	An abstract composition that perfectly balances color, shape, and texture to create visual harmony.
Balloon Art	A sculpture made entirely from twisted balloons, forming an intricate and colorful animal figure.

(continued)

Style Names	Description
Ballpoint Pen	A detailed portrait drawn with a ballpoint pen, showcasing intricate shading and textures.
Baroque	A dramatic painting full of emotion and movement, with rich colors and dramatic lighting typical of the Baroque period.
Baroque Art	An ornate church interior, depicted with attention to the lavish details and grandeur of Baroque architecture.
Bauhaus	A poster design featuring clean lines, primary colors, and geometric shapes, reflecting the Bauhaus design philosophy.
Bead Art	A portrait made from thousands of colored beads, meticulously placed to create depth and likeness.
Biomorphic Art	An abstract sculpture inspired by natural forms, with smooth, organic shapes suggesting growth and movement.
Blacklight Painting	A fluorescent mural that comes alive under blacklight, revealing hidden layers and vibrant colors.
Blueprint	A detailed architectural blueprint of a futuristic building, showing precise measurements and design concepts.
Body Art	A model covered in intricate body paint, transforming the human form into a living canvas.
Body Painting	A detailed scene painted across a group of bodies, creating a single cohesive image when viewed from a specific angle.
Book Cover	A captivating book cover design for a fantasy novel, featuring an enchanted forest and mystical creatures.

(continued)

Style Names	Description
Botanical Art	A detailed watercolor of a rare flower, scientifically accurate and beautifully rendered.
Botanical Illustration	An illustration of a medicinal plant, with labeled parts and detailed botanical accuracy.
Bronze Sculpture	A life-sized bronze statue of a dancer, capturing the fluidity and grace of the human form.
Bronze Statue	A heroic figure from mythology, cast in bronze, standing as a testament to strength and courage.
Bubble Wrap Painting	An abstract painting created by applying paint through bubble wrap, creating a unique texture and pattern.
Byzantine Icon	A religious icon painted in the Byzantine style, with gold leaf and solemn figures.
Calligraphy	A piece of calligraphy featuring an inspirational quote, with flowing letters and decorative flourishes.
Camel Bone Art	A finely carved camel bone, depicting a traditional scene with exquisite detail.
Camera Obscura	A photograph taken with a camera obscura, capturing a flipped and ethereal view of the outside world.
Caricature	A humorous caricature of a celebrity, exaggerating distinctive features for comic effect.
Cartoon	A fun, colorful cartoon strip telling a short, humorous story with engaging characters.
Carving	A detailed wood carving of a forest scene, with animals hidden among the trees and foliage.
Cave Painting	A modern interpretation of prehistoric cave paintings, featuring animals and symbols in earthy tones.

(continued)

Style Names	Description
Ceramics	A set of hand-thrown ceramic pots, glazed in harmonious colors and organic shapes.
CGI	A CGI image of a fantastical creature, rendered with lifelike detail and texture.
Chalk Drawing	A sidewalk chalk drawing that transforms the pavement into a vibrant, temporary artwork.
Chalk Pastel	A soft landscape rendered in chalk pastels, with gentle blending to capture the light and atmosphere.
Character	An original character design for a video game, detailed and ready for animation.
Charcoal	A dramatic charcoal drawing of a stormy sea, with dark, brooding tones and intense contrasts.
Charcoal Drawing	A portrait drawn in charcoal, capturing subtle expressions with soft shading and depth.
Children's Book Illustration	A bright, engaging illustration of animals having a picnic, perfect for a children's book.
Child's Drawing	A simple, joyful drawing by a child, featuring a sun, a house, and a family, full of imagination.
Chinese Art	A traditional Chinese painting of a bamboo grove, with delicate brushwork and ink washes.
Chinese Watercolor	A watercolor painting of a peony, using traditional Chinese techniques and symbolism.
Chromolithograph	A reproduction of a 19th-century chromolithograph, vibrant and detailed, showcasing the art of color printing.
Claymation	A frame from a claymation film, showing a clay character in a whimsically constructed set.

(continued)

Style Names	Description
Coffee Filter Art	Art created by staining coffee filters, arranged to form a large, colorful mosaic.
Coffee Painting	A painting made using coffee as the medium, creating sepia-toned images with varying shades.
Collage	A mixed-media collage incorporating vintage photos, paper textures, and handwritten notes.
Collage Of Magazine Cutouts	A portrait composed of magazine cutouts, creating a complex, layered effect.
Collage Painting	An artwork blending paint and collage techniques to create a textured, multifaceted composition.
Color Theory	An abstract painting exploring color relationships, with blocks of color interacting in visually compelling ways.
Colored Pencil	A detailed still life drawn with colored pencils, showing vibrant colors and fine textures.
Colorful Scribbles	A playful, abstract composition of colorful scribbles that overlap and intersect.
Colorful Spikey Hair	An illustration of a character with exaggerated, colorful spiky hair, bold and expressive.
Coloring-in Sheet	A detailed black and white illustration designed for coloring, featuring intricate patterns or scenes.
Comic Book Art	A dynamic comic book page, with bold illustrations and action-packed sequences.
Composition Art	An artwork carefully composed to guide the viewer's eye through color, shape, and balance.
Concept Art	A piece of concept art for a fantasy video game, showing a detailed environment or character.

(continued)

Style Names	Description
Conceptual Art	An art piece prioritizes the idea over the physical execution, challenging traditional notions of art.
Constructivism	An artwork inspired by Constructivism, with industrial materials and a focus on social function.
Contemporary Art	An installation piece that reflects on modern societal issues, using mixed media to provoke thought.
Courtroom Sketch	A quick sketch capturing a dramatic moment in a courtroom, conveying the tension and emotion of the scene.
Crayon	A vibrant landscape created with crayons, showcasing the medium's potential for texture and color blending.
Crayon Drawing	A whimsical drawing of a house and garden, rendered in the bright, waxy colors of crayons.
Creativity	An abstract representation of creativity, with swirling colors and forms suggesting the flow of ideas.
Crochet	A detailed crochet piece, forming an intricate pattern or image with yarn, warm and textured.
Cubism	A cubist portrait, breaking the subject into geometric shapes and reassembling them in abstract form.
Cyanotype	A cyanotype print of ferns, with the distinctive blue hue and delicate details of the process.
Cybernetic	An artwork depicting a cybernetic organism, blending organic and mechanical elements, futuristic and detailed.
Cyberpunk	A neon-lit cyberpunk streetscape, with towering skyscrapers and bustling crowds, immersive and detailed.

(continued)

Style Names	Description
Cyberpunk Art	A digital illustration of a cyberpunk character, with glowing neon accents and futuristic attire.
Dadaism	A collage made in the spirit of Dada, combining random images and text to challenge traditional art concepts.
Dashcam Video	A still from a dashcam video, capturing a fleeting, unexpected moment on the road, candid and raw.
De Stijl	An artwork inspired by De Stijl, focusing on horizontal and vertical lines and primary colors.
Decalcomania	A surreal, patterned artwork created by pressing paint between two surfaces, then pulling them apart.
Decorative Minoan Mural	A reproduction of a Minoan fresco, vibrant and detailed, depicting scenes from ancient Crete.
Decoupage	An object decorated with a decoupage, covered in cutouts from magazines or paper, sealed for a glossy finish.
Design	A sleek, modern design for a piece of furniture, combining functionality with aesthetic appeal.
Detail	A close-up painting focusing on the intricate details of a bird's feather, realistic and detailed.
Diagram	A clear, informative diagram explaining a scientific concept, with labels and concise descriptions.
Dieselpunk	An illustration in the dieselpunk genre, featuring retro-futuristic technology and art deco influences.
Digital Art	A vibrant, digital painting of an alien landscape, showcasing the possibilities of digital media.
Digital Painting	A detailed digital portrait, with rich textures and lifelike colors, created using a tablet and stylus.

(continued)

Style Names	Description
Digital Sculpting	A 3D model of a fantasy creature, sculpted digitally with attention to texture and form.
Disposable Camera	A photo capturing a spontaneous moment, taken with a disposable camera, nostalgic and grainy.
Doodle Art	A complex, intricate doodle covering an entire page, with patterns, characters, and abstract shapes.
Double Exposure	A photograph combining two images into one, creating a surreal and layered effect.
Drawing	A detailed pencil drawing of a quiet street scene, capturing the mood and textures with shading.
Dripping Paint	An abstract painting created by allowing paint to drip down the canvas, colorful and spontaneous.
Dutch Art	A still life painting in the style of the Dutch Golden Age, with rich details and dramatic lighting.
Early Renaissance Art	A painting depicting a religious scene, with careful attention to human anatomy and perspective.
Ebru (Turkish Marbling)	A traditional Ebru artwork, with swirling patterns of paint floating on water, transferred to paper.
Editorial Fashion Photography	A striking fashion photograph, telling a story with dramatic lighting and composition.
Editorial Illustration	An illustration accompanying a magazine article, visually interpreting the theme with creativity.
Eggshell Mosaic	A mosaic made from colored eggshell pieces, creating a delicate and detailed image.
Egyptian Art	A painting inspired by ancient Egyptian art, with profile figures, hieroglyphics, and symbolic imagery.

(continued)

165

Style Names	Description
Electrostatic Painting	A painting technique using electrostatically charged powder, resulting in a smooth, even coat.
Embroidery	A detailed embroidery piece, featuring a complex design stitched with vibrant threads.
Encaustic Painting	An artwork made with pigmented wax, layered and fused with heat for texture and depth.
Engraving	A finely detailed engraving on metal, depicting a landscape with precision and clarity.
Etching	An etching print of a hauntingly beautiful forest scene, with fine lines creating depth and shadow.
Etching Metal	A piece of metal etched with an intricate pattern, using acid to carve out the design.
Experimental Photography	A photograph using unconventional techniques, creating an abstract and captivating image.
Expressionism	A painting expressing raw emotions through distorted forms and explosive colors.
Fantasy	An illustration of a fantastical world, with dragons soaring over castles and enchanted forests.
Fashion Illustration	A stylized drawing of a fashion model, showcasing an avant-garde outfit with dynamic lines and colors.
Fauvism	A landscape painted with bold, unmodulated colors, capturing the essence rather than the reality.
Finger Painting	An abstract piece created with finger painting, showcasing the tactile joy and immediacy of the medium.
Fingerprint Art	Art made by using fingerprints to create playful characters and scenes, whimsical and personal.

(continued)

Style Names	Description
Folded Paper Art	An intricate design created by folding paper, resulting in geometric patterns and shapes.
Folk Art	A painting that embodies the simplicity and charm of traditional folk art, with bright colors and naive figures.
Fractal Art	A digital artwork made of fractals, with endlessly repeating patterns that create a mesmerizing effect.
Fresco	A mural painted on wet plaster in the fresco technique, vibrant and enduring.
Fresco Secco	A painting done on dry plaster, allowing for more detail but less durability than true fresco.
Full Body Photo	A photograph capturing the entire figure of a person, showcasing their attire and posture.
Fumage	Art created by holding paper over a flame and manipulating the smoke to create images, ethereal and ghostly.
Functional Art	A piece of art that serves a practical purpose, beautifully blending aesthetics with utility.
Futurism	An artwork capturing the dynamic energy of the future, with motion and modernity at its core.
Game Art	Concept art for a video game, detailing a character or scene, rich in imagination and detail.
Gargoyles	A sculpture of a gargoyle, combining grotesque features with architectural function, menacing and protective.
Geometric Abstraction	An abstract composition of geometric shapes, playing with form, color, and space.
Geometric Art	Art based on geometric shapes and patterns, creating a structured and harmonious visual effect.

(*continued*)

Style Names	Description
Glitch Art	An artwork that incorporates digital glitches, creating an intentionally disrupted and aesthetic visual.
Glitchcore Design	A design that embraces the aesthetics of digital errors, vibrant and chaotic.
Glitter and Glue Craft	A craft project using glitter and glue to create sparkly, decorative art, playful and bright.
Gongbi Painting	A Chinese painting characterized by meticulous brushwork and detailed depictions of figures or landscapes.
Gothic Design	An artwork featuring the pointed arches, ribbed vaults, and ornate detailing of Gothic architecture.
Gouache	A painting using gouache, a water-based medium known for its opacity and vibrant colors.
Graffiti	Urban art spray-painted on a wall, bold and expressive, with stylized lettering and images.
Graphic Design	A digital design that communicates a specific message through typography, color, and layout.
Graphic Novel Illustration	A panel from a graphic novel, combining narrative and artwork to tell a story.
Grayscale Photography	A black and white photograph that captures a range of grays, emphasizing texture and contrast.
Greek Art	A sculpture inspired by ancient Greek art, with idealized forms and a focus on human beauty and symmetry.
Grisaille Painting	A painting executed entirely in shades of gray, mimicking the sculpture's appearance.
Gyotaku Art	A traditional Japanese art form of fish printing, where a real fish is used to transfer its image to paper.

(*continued*)

Style Names	Description
Hand-Drawn Animation	A sequence of hand-drawn frames, creating the illusion of movement in an animated film.
Handprint Art	Art created using handprints as the main motif, fun and personal.
Haptic Art	Art that engages the sense of touch, inviting interaction and exploration beyond visual appreciation.
Hard-Edge Painting	An abstract painting with sharp, crisp edges between color areas, emphasizing clarity and precision.
Harsh Flash Photography	A photograph taken with harsh flash, creating dramatic shadows and a raw, candid feel.
Hieroglyphics	An artwork that incorporates ancient Egyptian hieroglyphics, mysterious and symbolic.
High Key Lighting	A photograph with high key lighting, creating a light, airy atmosphere with minimal shadows.
Houdini 3D Rendering	A complex 3D scene rendered in Houdini, showcasing advanced visual effects and simulations.
Hyperrealism Painting	A painting so detailed and lifelike, it resembles a high-resolution photograph.
Ice Carving	A sculpture carved from a block of ice, ephemeral and crystalline.
Ice Painting	Art created by painting with colored ice, resulting in fluid, melting patterns.
Illustration	A detailed illustration for a fantasy novel cover, capturing an epic scene with vibrant colors and dynamic composition.
Illustrator Software	A digital portrait of a person, using Adobe Illustrator, featuring smooth vector lines and gradients.

(*continued*)

Style Names	Description
Impasto Paint	A landscape painted with thick, textured layers of paint, giving a three-dimensional effect.
Impressionism	A painting capturing the fleeting effects of light on a scene, with quick brushstrokes and vibrant colors.
Impressionist Painting	A garden scene at sunset, with quick brush strokes and a focus on the effects of light on color.
Indian Art	A traditional Rajasthani painting, featuring intricate patterns and bold colors.
Indian Art Painting	A scene from the Mahabharata, rich in detail and symbolism, using vibrant colors.
Ink Art	A detailed ink drawing of an intricate mandala, showcasing precision and pattern.
Ink Wash Painting	A minimalist landscape, using varying ink concentrations to create depth and perspective.
Installation Art	An immersive installation that transforms a space, creating an interactive experience for viewers.
Instruction Manual Design	A clear, visually guided manual for assembling a complex gadget, with detailed diagrams.
Interior Design	A modern living room layout, with sleek furniture and a harmonious color palette.
Japanese Art	A serene ink-wash painting of Mount Fuji, focusing on simplicity and negative space.
Jelly Bean Art	A portrait made entirely of jellybeans, colorful and playful, showcasing a creative use of materials.
Juxtaposition	Art that places contrasting elements side by side, highlighting their differences and creating a striking effect.

(continued)

Style Names	Description
Kindergartener Drawing	A simple, joyful depiction of a family, with bright colors and exaggerated features.
Kinetic Art	A sculpture that moves with the wind, creating an ever-changing pattern of shadows.
Kinetic Painting	A canvas incorporating moving parts, creating an artwork that evolves over time.
Kirigami	A detailed paper cut-out of a snowflake, intricate and symmetrical.
Kitsch Art	A velvet painting of a unicorn in a neon landscape, playful and exaggerated.
Knitting Fiber Art	A large, textured wall hanging, knitted with various yarns and colors.
Land Art	A geometric pattern created in a desert landscape, using stones and sand.
Landscape Painting	A tranquil scene of a mountain lake at dawn, with reflections in the water.
Layered Paper Art	A 3D portrait made from cut and layered colored paper, detailed and vibrant.
Light Art	An installation using projected lights to create an abstract, immersive experience.
Lighting	A photograph capturing the dramatic play of sunlight through a forest canopy.
Line Art	A minimalist drawing of a cat, using a single, unbroken line.
Line Art Painting	An abstract composition made of straight and curved lines, black on white.

(*continued*)

Style Names	Description
Line Drawing	A detailed sketch of a city skyline, focusing on architectural details.
Linocut Printmaking	A bold, graphic print of a bird, with strong contrasts and textures.
Lithography	A fine art print of a landscape, with subtle gradations and rich tones.
Lomography	A dreamy, saturated photo of a carnival at night, taken with a Lomo camera.
Long Exposure Photography	A silky waterfall surrounded by autumn leaves, captured with a slow shutter speed.
Looney Tunes Art Style	A playful drawing of Bugs Bunny, in the classic animation style.
Low Poly	A digital art piece of a fox, made from geometric shapes, simple and modern.
Lowbrow Pop Surrealism	An imaginative scene featuring a girl riding a giant rabbit, whimsical and slightly eerie.
Luminism Landscape	A painting capturing the subtle effects of light on a river scene, serene and detailed.
Macchiaioli Painting	An outdoor scene with dappled light filtering through trees, using quick, visible brushstrokes.
Macramé Fiber Art	A hanging planter made from knotted cords, intricate and bohemian.
Macro Photography	A close-up photo of a dewdrop on a spiderweb, detailed and crisp.
Mandalas	A complex, symmetrical design using vibrant colors and patterns, meditative and detailed.

(continued)

Style Names	Description
Manga	A dynamic comic panel featuring a hero in mid-action, expressive and stylized.
Mannerism Art	An elongated portrait of a noble, with exaggerated proportions and elegant poses.
Manuscript Illumination	A page from a medieval book, decorated with gold leaf and miniature illustrations.
Marble Sculpture	A classical figure, carved with lifelike details and smooth finishes.
Marker Rendering	A colorful illustration of a tropical bird, vibrant and detailed.
Mathematical Art	A 3D printed sculpture based on a complex mathematical equation, intricate and abstract.
Matte Painting	A digital artwork of an alien landscape, realistic and detailed, for a movie scene.
Medieval Art	A religious icon, with gold backgrounds and symbolic imagery, solemn and ornate.
Medieval Portrait	A nobleman, depicted with a richly detailed cloak and a solemn expression.
Melted Crayon Art	A canvas with brightly colored crayons melted and dripped to create an abstract piece.
Mexican Muralism	A large wall painting depicting a historical scene, bold and socially charged.
Minimalism	A simple, geometric composition, using a limited color palette and clean lines.
Minimalist Art	An artwork focusing on simplicity and negative space, with a single, impactful element.

(*continued*)

173

Style Names	Description
Mixed Media	A collage combining paint, fabric, and found objects, textured and layered.
Modeling Photoshoot	A fashion model posed against a minimalist backdrop, stylish and polished.
Modern Art	An abstract painting with bold shapes and colors, challenging traditional forms.
Monochromatic	An artwork using shades of a single color, creating depth and interest with minimal hues.
Monochrome	A black and white photograph of an urban scene, dramatic and timeless.
Monoprinting	A unique print made by drawing on a plate, with expressive lines and textures.
Moo Card Paintings	Tiny, business card-sized paintings, detailed and collectible.
Mosaic	A colorful design created with small tiles, detailed and vibrant.
Mugshot	A stylized portrait inspired by vintage criminal mugshots, gritty and intriguing.
Mural Art	A community-inspired painting on a large public wall, vibrant and engaging.
Mythological Art	A depiction of a Greek god, dramatic and filled with symbolic elements.
Naïve Art	A painting of a village scene, with a childlike perspective and bright colors.
Negative Space	An illustration where the space around the subject forms an interesting shape, clever and minimalist.

(continued)

Style Names	Description
Neoclassicism	A painting inspired by ancient Greek and Roman art, with idealized figures and clear forms.
Neon Art	A sculpture made from neon tubes, glowing and contemporary.
New Media Art	An interactive digital installation, responsive and immersive.
Oil Painting	A portrait with rich textures and depth, capturing the subtle nuances of light.
One-line Drawing	An animal drawn without lifting the pen from the paper, minimalist and fluid.
Op Art	An abstract design that creates an optical illusion of movement, black and white and mesmerizing.
Optical Art	A canvas pulsing with geometric patterns, vibrant and eye-catching.
Oriental Art	A delicate ink painting of a cherry blossom branch, traditional and elegant.
Origami	A complex paper crane, folded from a single sheet of paper, precise and delicate.
Orphism	An abstract composition with overlapping, translucent circles of color, vibrant and rhythmic.
Painting	A landscape capturing the changing colors of autumn, rich and immersive.
Paper Cutouts	A scene created from layered paper cutouts, detailed and shadowed.
Paper Cutting	A delicate pattern cut from black paper, intricate and lace-like.

(*continued*)

Style Names	Description
Paper Mache	A whimsical sculpture of a fantastical creature, colorful and textured.
Paper Quilling	A floral design made from rolled and shaped paper strips, detailed and three-dimensional.
Pastel Drawing	A soft, dreamy seascape at dusk, with gentle colors blending smoothly.
Patent Drawing	A technical illustration of a new invention, detailed and precise.
Pattern	A repeating geometric design, bold and modern.
Pen and Ink	A detailed architectural sketch of an old building, precise and intricate.
Pencil and Watercolor Drawing	A bird illustrated in pencil, with a watercolor wash for vibrancy.
Pencil Drawing	A realistic portrait, with detailed shading and lifelike textures.
Pencil Sketching	A quick sketch of a bustling café scene, lively and expressive.
Performance Art	An artist creating a live painting, surrounded by an audience, dynamic and engaging.
Photo-bashing	A concept art piece for a video game, combining photography and digital painting.
Photograph	A candid shot of a city street at night, illuminated by street lamps, atmospheric and moody.
Photography	A landscape photo capturing the grandeur of a mountain range, majestic and sweeping.

(continued)

Style Names	Description
Photorealism	A painting of a diner that looks nearly identical to a photograph, detailed and glossy.
Photoshopped Image	A fantastical creature, digitally created by combining elements of various animals.
Pietra Dura	An intricate inlay of semi-precious stones on a tabletop, detailed and colorful.
Pinhole Photography	A dreamy landscape captured with a pinhole camera, soft and ethereal.
Pixel Art	A character from a classic video game, nostalgic and blocky.
Playdough Creations	A whimsical scene made entirely from colorful playdough, playful and textured.
Pointillism	A park scene made from thousands of tiny dots, vibrant and shimmering.
Polaroid	A vintage-style photo of friends laughing, spontaneous and nostalgic.
Pop Art	A bold portrait of a celebrity, using bright colors and pop culture references.
Portrait Art	An expressive painting of a person, capturing their essence and emotion.
Portrait Painting	A detailed oil painting of an elderly man, with every wrinkle telling a story.
Post Impressionism	A landscape with exaggerated colors and brush strokes, emotional and vibrant.
Post-Apocalyptic	A digital painting of a deserted city, overgrown and mysterious.

(continued)

177

Style Names	Description
Postmodern Art	A sculpture combining industrial materials and classical forms, challenging and ironic.
Potato Stamp Printing	A series of prints made with potato stamps, simple and folk-art inspired.
Poured Paint Art	An abstract canvas with layers of poured paint, creating a fluid, marbled effect.
Prehistoric Art	A cave painting depicting ancient hunting scenes, primitive and powerful.
Press Release	A visually engaging announcement for an art exhibit, combining text and imagery.
Printmaking	A limited edition linocut print of a forest, stark and stylized.
Product Photography	A sleek photo of a new smartphone, highlighting its design and features.
Professional Corporate Portrait	A headshot of a CEO, polished and commanding.
Psychedelic Art	A poster for a music festival, with swirling colors and trippy designs.
Puffed Paint	A tactile painting on fabric, with raised designs that pop off the surface.
Quilling	A delicate design of flowers made from coiled paper strips, intricate and colorful.
Quilting	A patchwork quilt with a complex geometric pattern, cozy and handcrafted.
Raster Design	A digital landscape illustration, rich in textures and gradients.

(continued)

Style Names	Description
Real Estate Photography	A photo showcasing the spacious interior of a modern home, inviting and bright.
Realism	A still life painting so detailed it looks like a photograph, rich and textured.
Renaissance	A painting of a mythological scene, with balanced composition and humanist ideals.
Retro	A poster design inspired by the 1960s, with bold typography and psychedelic colors.
Retro Pixel Art	A scene from an 8-bit video game, nostalgic and pixelated.
Reverse Glass Painting	A floral design painted on the back of glass, vibrant and glossy.
Rick and Morty Art Style	A chaotic scene featuring the show's characters on an interdimensional adventure, vibrant and exaggerated.
Rococo	An ornate interior scene, with delicate furniture and pastel colors, lavish and elegant.
Roman Mosaic	A floor mosaic depicting a mythological battle, detailed and historic.
Romanticism	A dramatic landscape with towering mountains and a stormy sky, emotive and sublime.
Rorschach Art	An inkblot design, symmetrical and open to interpretation.
Sand Animation	A performance creating changing pictures with sand, ephemeral and captivating.
Sand Art	A detailed sculpture made from sand, temporary and intricate.
Sand Painting	A traditional Navajo sand painting, symbolic and ceremonial.

(continued)

Style Names	Description
Sci-fi Art	A digital painting of a space station orbiting an alien planet, futuristic and detailed.
Scratchboard	An image of a tiger, etched into a scratchboard, revealing white lines on a black background, detailed and contrasted.
Sculpture	A modern abstract sculpture in metal, dynamic and reflective.
Selfies	A creative selfie with dramatic lighting and an interesting background, personal and expressive.
Seurat Pointillism	A park scene, composed entirely of small, distinct dots of color, vibrant and optical.
Sfumato	A portrait with soft, blurred edges, creating a smoky effect, subtle and mysterious.
Sgraffito	A ceramic plate with a design etched through a top layer of glaze, revealing the contrasting color beneath, textured and decorative.
Shading	A drawing focusing on the use of light and shadow to create depth, realistic and dimensional.
Shadow Art	An installation where objects are arranged to cast a recognizable shadow, clever and transformative.
Shadow Puppetry	A performance with cut-out figures held against a lit backdrop, creating moving silhouettes, traditional and storytelling.
Shot on iPhone	A stunning landscape shot with an iPhone, showcasing the device's camera capabilities, crisp and vibrant.
Sidewalk Chalk Art	A 3D illusion created with chalk on the pavement, interactive and colorful.

(*continued*)

Style Names	Description
Silhouette Painting	A minimalist silhouette of a cityscape against a sunset, stark and simple.
Sketch	A quick pencil sketch of a bustling street scene, lively and gestural.
Sketchbook	A page from a sketchbook filled with various doodles and ideas, personal and creative.
Skeuomorphism	A digital interface design that mimics the physical world, detailed and realistic.
Social Realism	A painting depicting the struggles of the working class, poignant and empathetic.
South Park Art Style	A scene with characters in the show's simple, cut-out style, satirical and bold.
Spanish Art	A flamenco dancer painted in a vibrant, expressive style, passionate and lively.
Spirograph	A design created with a spirograph, intricate and geometric.
Surrealism	A scene where dreamlike elements blend with reality, imaginative and bizarre.
Symbolism	An artwork rich in symbolic imagery, open to interpretation, deep and meaningful.
Synthwave	A digital artwork capturing the neon aesthetics of the 80s, vibrant and nostalgic.
Tattoo Art	A detailed sketch of a traditional tattoo design, bold and iconic.
Terracotta Warriors	A detailed clay sculpture modeled after the ancient Chinese terracotta soldiers, historic and lifelike.

(continued)

Style Names	Description
Textile Art	A tapestry featuring an abstract design, rich in texture and color.
Texture	A close-up photograph emphasizing the texture of a leaf, detailed and macro.
Theatrical Press Release	A visually striking poster for a theater production, combining text and imagery, enticing and dramatic.
Thermochromic Painting	Artwork that changes color with temperature, interactive and dynamic.
Tie-dye	A fabric piece showcasing a vibrant tie-dye pattern, colorful and psychedelic.
Topiary	A photograph of a garden with bushes sculpted into artistic shapes, green and sculptural.
Trompe-l'œil	A painting that creates the optical illusion of three-dimensional space on a flat surface realistic and deceptive.
Typography	A design focusing on creative letterforms, engaging and artistic.
Ukiyo-e	A woodblock print of a historical Japanese scene, detailed and traditional.
Under Electron Microscope	An image showing the intricate structure of a crystal, magnified and detailed.
Unity3D Art	A screenshot from a 3D game developed in Unity showcasing detailed environments and characters.
Upcycling	A piece of furniture creatively repurposed from old materials, sustainable and innovative.
UV Painting	Artwork that reveals hidden details under UV light, mysterious and glowing.

(*continued*)

Style Names	Description
Vector Art	A digital illustration made with vector software, clean and scalable.
Watercolor Painting	A landscape painted with watercolors, capturing the fluidity and translucence of the medium.
Weaving	A handwoven textile with an intricate pattern, textured and colorful.
Wet-on-Wet Oil Painting	A technique where layers of wet paint are applied over wet paint, creating a soft, blended effect.
Wire Sculpture	A delicate sculpture made from intricate and metallic twisted wire forms the shape of a tree.
Wood Carving	A detailed carving of an animal showcasing the wood's natural grain, textured and rustic.
Woodcut	A print made from a carved wooden block, stark and graphic.
Yarn Art	A piece of art is created by wrapping colored yarn around nails on a board, creating geometric patterns that are vibrant and textured.

APPENDIX B

A Giant List of Textures

Use the following texture names to spice up your images.

Abrasive	Dotted	Glossy	Layered	Multi-layered	Silty	Tangled
Absorbent	Downy	Gluey	Leafy	Mushy	Simple	Taut
Artificial	Draped	Gnarled	Leathery	Natural	Sinewy	Tender
Asymmetrical	Drenched	Gooey	Light	Nebulous	Sleek	Terraced
Baked	Dripping	Grainy	Limber	Needle-like	Slimy	Textured
Banded	Dry	Granular	Lined	Netted	Slippery	Thick
Barbed	Dull	Grassy	Liquid	Non-slip	Slithery	Thin
Barren	Dusty	Greasy	Lumpy	Notched	Sloshy	Thorny
Beaded	Elastic	Gritty	Luminous	Oily	Smooth	Threaded
Blistered	Embossed	Grooved	Luxurious	Open	Smudgy	Tight
Bloated	Engraved	Gummy	Magnetic	Ornate	Snowy	Tiled
Blotchy	Etched	Hairy	Malleable	Padded	Soapy	Tinny
Blurred	Even	Hard	Marbled	Painted	Soft	Tiny
Boiling	Expansive	Harsh	Marshy	Papery	Solid	Toasty
Bouncy	Feathery	Heavy	Matte	Parched	Spongy	Torn
Braided	Fibrous	Honeycombed	Meandering	Patterned	Springy	Translucent

Bristled	Filmy	Icy	Metallic	Pebbled	Squishy	Transparent
Bubbly	Fine	Illuminated	Mildewed	Perforated	Stable	Treacherous
Bumpy	Firm	Impenetrable	Milky	Permeable	Stained	Tree-like
Buoyant	Fissured	Impervious	Mirrored	Pitted	Starched	Trimmed
Bushy	Flaky	Inflated	Misty	Plaited	Sticky	Twisted
Buttery	Flat	Interwoven	Moist	Plastic	Stiff	Uneven
Caked	Fleecy	Irregular	Molded	Plated	Still	Unglossy
Calcified	Fleshy	Jagged	Mossy	Pliable	Stony	Unique
Carved	Flexible	Knitted	Muddy	Plucked	Straight	Unpolished
Chalky	Flimsy	Knobbly	Muffled	Plush	Stretchy	Unrefined
Charred	Fluffy	Knotted	Multi-layered	Polished	Striated	Unsmooth
Chipped	Foamy	Lacquered	Mushy	Porous	Striped	Untamed
Chiseled	Folded	Layered	Natural	Prickly	Strong	Velvety
Clumpy	Fragile	Leafy	Nebulous	Puffy	Structured	Vibrant
Clustered	Frayed	Leathery	Needle-like	Pulpy	Stubbly	Viscous
Coarse	Frigid	Light	Netted	Pungent	Stuffed	Vitreous

(continued)

187

APPENDIX B   A GIANT LIST OF TEXTURES

Cold	Frosted	Limber	Non-slip	Quilted	Sturdy	Vivid
Compact	Frosty	Lined	Notched	Radiant	Suave	Waxy
Complex	Furry	Liquid	Oily	Ragged	Sudsy	Webbed
Compressed	Fuzzy	Lumpy	Open	Rainy	Sugary	Wet
Concave	Gaseous	Luminous	Ornate	Raspy	Sunken	Whirled
Concrete	Gelatinous	Luxurious	Padded	Rattling	Supple	Wiry
Convoluted	Gilded	Magnetic	Painted	Reflective	Swirled	Withered
Cool	Glistening	Marshy	Papery	Reflective	Tacky	Woody
Corrugated	Glittery	Glossy	Matted	Resilient	Tangy	Woolly
Cracked	Gloopy	Gluey	Matte	Ribbed	Tangled	Woven
Cratered	Glossy	Gnarled	Metallic	Rigid	Taut	Wrinkled
Creamy	Gooey	Granular	Mildewed	Rippled	Tender	Yielding
Crinkled	Grainy	Grassy	Milky	Rough	Terraced	Zesty
Crispy	Granular	Greasy	Mirrored	Rugged	Textured	Zigzagged

APPENDIX C

Prompts to Demonstrate Artists' Styles

Use these prompt starters to demonstrate known styles of various artists.

Style	Artist	Midjourney v 6.0 prompt to demonstrate the style
Abstract Collage	Kurt Schwitters	Abstract Collage - Kurt Schwitters - Kurt Schwitters' abstract collage, a fusion of found materials in a fragmented visual language. --v 6.0
Abstract Expressionism	Willem de Kooning	Abstract Expressionism - Willem de Kooning - Willem de Kooning's dynamic abstract expressionist painting, known for its powerful brushwork and emotional depth. --v 6.0

(*continued*)

© The Editor(s) (if applicable) and The Author(s),
under exclusive license to APress Media, LLC, part of Springer Nature 2024
I. Shamaeva, *Advanced Styles and Insights with Midjourney*,
https://doi.org/10.1007/979-8-8688-0336-9

Style	Artist	Midjourney v 6.0 prompt to demonstrate the style
Abstract Expressionist	Helen Frankenthaler	Abstract Expressionist - Helen Frankenthaler - Helen Frankenthaler, an abstract expressionist, known for her innovative 'soak-stain' technique. --v 6.0
Abstract Expressionist	Lee Krasner	Abstract Expressionist - Lee Krasner - Lee Krasner, an abstract expressionist, expressed her inner world through bold and dynamic compositions. --v 6.0
Abstract Expressionist Sculpture	David Smith	Abstract Expressionist Sculpture - David Smith - David Smith's abstract expressionist sculpture, bold and dynamic metal constructions. --v 6.0
Abstract Figurative	Francis Bacon	Abstract Figurative - Francis Bacon - Francis Bacon's abstract figurative art, distorted and emotionally charged depictions of the human form. --v 6.0
Abstract Impressionism	Joan Mitchell	Abstract Impressionism - Joan Mitchell - Joan Mitchell's abstract impressionism, a vivid canvas of emotional brushwork and color exploration. --v 6.0
Abstract Pop Art	Roy Lichtenstein	Abstract Pop Art - Roy Lichtenstein - Roy Lichtenstein's abstract pop art, transforming everyday objects into bold and colorful abstractions. --v 6.0

(*continued*)

Style	Artist	Midjourney v 6.0 prompt to demonstrate the style
Abstract Realism	Chuck Close	Abstract Realism - Chuck Close - Chuck Close's abstract realism, intricate portraits composed of intricate patterns of color and shape. --v 6.0
Abstract Realist	Mark Rothko	Abstract Realist - Mark Rothko - Mark Rothko, an abstract realist, used color to evoke deep emotional responses in his viewers. --v 6.0
Abstract Romanticism	William Turner	Abstract Romanticism - William Turner - William Turner's abstract romanticism, capturing the emotional power of nature in swirling colors. --v 6.0
Abstract Surrealism	Yves Tanguy	Abstract Surrealism - Yves Tanguy - Yves Tanguy's abstract surrealism, a world of dreamlike landscapes and strange, organic forms. --v 6.0
Abstract Symbolism	Wassily Kandinsky	Abstract Symbolism - Wassily Kandinsky - Wassily Kandinsky's abstract symbolism, where colors and shapes convey deep emotional and spiritual meanings. --v 6.0
Abstract Visionary	Kazimir Malevich	Abstract Visionary - Kazimir Malevich - Kazimir Malevich, an abstract visionary, pioneered suprematism with simple geometric shapes. --v 6.0

(continued)

191

Style	Artist	Midjourney v 6.0 prompt to demonstrate the style
Action Painting	Jackson Pollock	Action Painting - Jackson Pollock - Jackson Pollock splatter painting in his signature energetic abstract expressionist style. --v 6.0
Aerosolgrafia	Banksy	Aerosolgrafia - Banksy - A Banksy style aerosol graffiti artwork of a girl releasing red balloons. --v 6.0
Analytical Cubism	Juan Gris	Analytical Cubism - Juan Gris - Juan Gris' analytical cubism, precise deconstruction of objects into geometric forms. --v 6.0
Anamorphic Art	István Orosz	Anamorphic Art - István Orosz - Mind bending anamorphic surrealist artwork in the style of István Orosz. --v 6.0
Art Brut	Jean Dubuffet	Art Brut - Jean Dubuffet - Jean Dubuffet's art brut, raw and unrefined art created outside the traditional art world. --v 6.0
Art Brut Sculpture	Gaston Chaissac	Art Brut Sculpture - Gaston Chaissac - Gaston Chaissac's art brut sculpture, celebrating the untamed creativity of outsider art. --v 6.0
Art Deco	Tamara de Lempicka	Art Deco - Tamara de Lempicka - Tamara de Lempicka's art deco masterpiece, characterized by sleek lines and glamorous elegance. --v 6.0

(continued)

Style	Artist	Midjourney v 6.0 prompt to demonstrate the style
Art Informel	Alberto Burri	Art Informel - Alberto Burri - Alberto Burri's art informel, raw and gestural expressions using unconventional materials. --v 6.0
Art Nouveau	Alphonse Mucha	Art Nouveau - Alphonse Mucha - Alphonse Mucha's art nouveau masterpiece, characterized by flowing lines and intricate ornamentation. --v 6.0
Arte Povera	Michelangelo Pistoletto	Arte Povera - Michelangelo Pistoletto - Sculpture made from poor materials by Michelangelo Pistoletto arte povera style. --v 6.0
Assemblage Art	Joseph Cornell	Assemblage Art - Joseph Cornell - Assemblage box sculpture reminiscent of Joseph Cornell's dreamlike found object compositions. --v 6.0
Automatism	André Masson	Automatism - André Masson - Surreal sand painting with automatic drawing in the style of André Masson. --v 6.0
Baroque	Peter Paul Rubens	Baroque - Peter Paul Rubens - Peter Paul Rubens' baroque masterpiece, a celebration of dynamic composition and rich, dramatic color. --v 6.0

(continued)

Style	Artist	Midjourney v 6.0 prompt to demonstrate the style
Baroque Genius	Caravaggio	Baroque Genius - Caravaggio - Caravaggio, a baroque genius, revolutionized painting with dramatic use of light and shadow. --v 6.0
Baroque Genius	Rembrandt	Baroque Genius - Rembrandt - Rembrandt, a baroque genius, captured the human soul through his masterful use of light and shadow. --v 6.0
Biomorphic Art	Jean Arp	Biomorphic Art - Jean Arp - Abstract bronze sculpture of a biomorphic shape by Jean Arp. --v 6.0
Blacklight Painting	Aaron De La Cruz	Blacklight Painting - Aaron De La Cruz - Ultraviolet blacklight painting of patterns and shapes by Aaron De La Cruz. --v 6.0
Body Painting	Craig Tracy	Body Painting - Craig Tracy - Body painting illusion on a female model in Craig Tracy's style. --v 6.0
Chiaroscuro	Caravaggio	Chiaroscuro - Caravaggio - Dramatic baroque oil painting Portrait of a Man Lit From The Side in Caravaggio's tenebrism style. --v 6.0
Color Field Abstraction	Barnett Newman	Color Field Abstraction - Barnett Newman - Barnett Newman's color field abstraction, large canvases dominated by bold, pure color fields. --v 6.0

(continued)

Style	Artist	Midjourney v 6.0 prompt to demonstrate the style
Color Field Painting	Mark Rothko	Color Field Painting - Mark Rothko - Mark Rothko's immersive color field painting, where large blocks of color evoke deep emotional responses. --v 6.0
Colorist	Sonia Delaunay	Colorist - Sonia Delaunay - Sonia Delaunay's colorist artwork, a vibrant explosion of geometric patterns and bold hues. --v 6.0
Colorist Painter	Howard Hodgkin	Colorist Painter - Howard Hodgkin - Howard Hodgkin, a colorist painter, used rich and vivid hues to evoke emotion and memory. --v 6.0
Colorist Painter	Pierre Bonnard	Colorist Painter - Pierre Bonnard - Pierre Bonnard, a colorist painter, used vibrant hues to infuse his scenes with warmth and intimacy. --v 6.0
Conceptual Art	Sol LeWitt	Conceptual Art - Sol LeWitt - Sol LeWitt's conceptual art, emphasizing ideas and systems in minimalist and geometric forms. --v 6.0
Conceptual Sculpture	Joseph Kosuth	Conceptual Sculpture - Joseph Kosuth - Joseph Kosuth's conceptual sculpture, exploring the relationship between language and art. --v 6.0

(continued)

195

Style	Artist	Midjourney v 6.0 prompt to demonstrate the style
Concrete Art	Max Bill	Concrete Art - Max Bill - Max Bill's concrete art, pure and precise geometric compositions exploring harmony and proportion. --v 6.0
Constructivism	Vladimir Tatlin	Constructivism - Vladimir Tatlin - Vladimir Tatlin's constructivist sculpture, a fusion of art and engineering that embodies revolutionary ideals. --v 6.0
Cubism	Pablo Picasso	Cubism - Pablo Picasso - Pablo Picasso's groundbreaking cubist artwork, featuring fragmented forms and a deconstruction of reality. --v 6.0
Cubist Artist	Fernand Léger	Cubist Artist - Fernand Léger - Fernand Léger, a cubist artist, merged elements of cubism and expressionism in his dynamic compositions. --v 6.0
Cubist Collage	Georges Braque	Cubist Collage - Georges Braque - Georges Braque's cubist collage, a revolutionary exploration of space and perception. --v 6.0
Cubist Sculpture	Alexander Archipenko	Cubist Sculpture - Alexander Archipenko - Alexander Archipenko's innovative cubist sculpture, a three-dimensional exploration of fragmented forms. --v 6.0

(*continued*)

Style	Artist	Midjourney v 6.0 prompt to demonstrate the style
Cubo-Expressionism	Fernand Léger	Cubo-Expressionism - Fernand Léger - Fernand Léger's cubo-expressionist artwork, combining elements of both cubism and expressionism. --v 6.0
Cubo-Futurism	Kazimir Malevich	Cubo-Futurism - Kazimir Malevich - Kazimir Malevich's innovative cubo-futurist artwork, merging the dynamic energy of futurism with cubist aesthetics. --v 6.0
Dadaism	Marcel Duchamp	Dadaism - Marcel Duchamp - Marcel Duchamp's dadaist readymade, challenging the traditional notions of art and the mundane. --v 6.0
Expressionist Painter	Egon Schiele	Expressionist Painter - Egon Schiele - Egon Schiele, an expressionist painter, conveyed raw emotion and vulnerability in his art. --v 6.0
Fantastic Realism	Ernst Fuchs	Fantastic Realism - Ernst Fuchs - Ernst Fuchs' fantastic realism, otherworldly and mystical paintings with intricate details. --v 6.0
Fauvism	Henri Matisse	Fauvism - Henri Matisse - Henri Matisse's fauvist masterpiece, where vibrant colors collide to create an explosion of visual intensity. --v 6.0

(continued)

197

Style	Artist	Midjourney v 6.0 prompt to demonstrate the style
Futurist Sculpture	Umberto Boccioni	Futurist Sculpture - Umberto Boccioni - Umberto Boccioni's futurist sculpture, embodying movement, speed, and the dynamism of modern life. --v 6.0
Geometric Abstraction	Kazimir Malevich	Geometric Abstraction - Kazimir Malevich - Kazimir Malevich's geometric abstraction, where perfect shapes and pure colors create visual harmony. --v 6.0
Geometric Expressionism	Kazuo Shiraga	Geometric Expressionism - Kazuo Shiraga - Kazuo Shiraga's geometric expressionism, bold and vibrant canvases created with the artist's own body. --v 6.0
Graffiti Art	Jean-Michel Basquiat	Graffiti Art - Jean-Michel Basquiat - Jean-Michel Basquiat's graffiti art, a raw and urban expression of social and personal themes. --v 6.0
Graffuturism	RETNA	Graffuturism - RETNA - RETNA's graffuturism, a fusion of graffiti and futurism, creating a unique visual language. --v 6.0
Hyperrealist Collage	Robert Bechtle	Hyperrealist Collage - Robert Bechtle - Robert Bechtle's hyperrealist collage, suburban scenes composed of meticulously cut and pasted details. --v 6.0

(continued)

Style	Artist	Midjourney v 6.0 prompt to demonstrate the style
Hyperrealist Sculpture	Ron Mueck	Hyperrealist Sculpture - Ron Mueck - Ron Mueck's hyperrealist sculpture, astonishingly lifelike and meticulously detailed. --v 6.0
Impressionist Painter	Berthe Morisot	Impressionist Painter - Berthe Morisot - Berthe Morisot, an impressionist painter, portrayed delicate scenes with a focus on light and color. --v 6.0
Impressionist Sculpture	Edgar Degas	Impressionist Sculpture - Edgar Degas - Edgar Degas' impressionist sculpture, capturing fleeting moments of grace and movement. --v 6.0
Kinetic Sculpture	Alexander Calder	Kinetic Sculpture - Alexander Calder - Alexander Calder's kinetic sculpture, where movement and balance merge in delicate harmony. --v 6.0
Magic Realism	Giorgio de Chirico	Magic Realism - Giorgio de Chirico - Giorgio de Chirico's magic realism, enigmatic and dreamlike cityscapes with a sense of mystery. --v 6.0
Magical Realism	Remedios Varo	Magical Realism - Remedios Varo - Remedios Varo's magical realism, blending fantasy and reality in mysterious and enchanting worlds. --v 6.0

(continued)

Style	Artist	Midjourney v 6.0 prompt to demonstrate the style
Modernist Master	Piet Mondrian	Modernist Master - Piet Mondrian - Piet Mondrian, a modernist master, reduced art to its essential elements with geometric forms and primary colors. --v 6.0
Naïve Art	Henri Rousseau	Naïve Art - Henri Rousseau - Henri Rousseau's naïve art, characterized by its childlike simplicity and vivid imagination. --v 6.0
Neo-Conceptual Sculpture	Rachel Whiteread	Neo-Conceptual Sculpture - Rachel Whiteread - Rachel Whiteread's neo-conceptual sculpture, transforming negative spaces into tangible objects. --v 6.0
Neo-Conceptualism	Jenny Holzer	Neo-Conceptualism - Jenny Holzer - Jenny Holzer's neo-conceptual art, using language and text to provoke thought and emotion. --v 6.0
Neo-Dada	Jasper Johns	Neo-Dada - Jasper Johns - Jasper Johns' neo-dada artwork, blurring the lines between art and everyday objects with his flag-inspired compositions. --v 6.0
Neo-Expressionism	Jean-Michel Basquiat	Neo-Expressionism - Jean-Michel Basquiat - Raw and energetic neo-expressionist artwork by Jean-Michel Basquiat with bold strokes and symbolic motifs. --v 6.0

(continued)

Style	Artist	Midjourney v 6.0 prompt to demonstrate the style
Neo-Expressionism	Joan Mitchell	Neo-Expressionism - Joan Mitchell - Joan Mitchell's abstract impressionism, a vivid canvas of emotional brushwork and color exploration. --v 6.0
Neo-Expressionist	Jean-Michel Basquiat	Neo-Expressionist - Jean-Michel Basquiat - Jean-Michel Basquiat, a neo-expressionist, conveyed raw energy and social commentary through his art. --v 6.0
Neo-Geo	Peter Halley	Neo-Geo - Peter Halley - Peter Halley's neo-geo artwork, exploring the juxtaposition of geometric forms and social commentary. --v 6.0
Neo-Geo Sculpture	Sarah Lucas	Neo-Geo Sculpture - Sarah Lucas - Sarah Lucas' neo-geo sculpture, provocative and subversive explorations of the human body. --v 6.0
Neo-Plasticism	Piet Mondrian	Neo-Plasticism - Piet Mondrian - Piet Mondrian's neo-plasticism, reducing art to its essential geometric elements with primary colors. --v 6.0
Neo-Pop	Jeff Koons	Neo-Pop - Jeff Koons - Jeff Koons' neo-pop art, turning everyday objects into larger-than-life icons. --v 6.0
Neo-Symbolism	Odd Nerdrum	Neo-Symbolism - Odd Nerdrum - Odd Nerdrum's neo-symbolism, haunting and enigmatic narratives in meticulously painted detail. --v 6.0

(continued)

Style	Artist	Midjourney v 6.0 prompt to demonstrate the style
New Objectivity	Otto Dix	New Objectivity - Otto Dix - Otto Dix's new objectivity, stark and unflinching portrayals of the harsh realities of post-war Germany. --v 6.0
Op Art	Bridget Riley	Op Art - Bridget Riley - Bridget Riley's mesmerizing op art piece, characterized by optical illusions and vibrant geometric patterns. --v 6.0
Op Art Sculpture	Victor Vasarely	Op Art Sculpture - Victor Vasarely - Victor Vasarely's op art sculpture, creating optical illusions through geometric arrangements. --v 6.0
Optical Sculpture	Yaacov Agam	Optical Sculpture - Yaacov Agam - Yaacov Agam's optical sculpture, an interactive and kinetic exploration of perception. --v 6.0
Orientalism	Eugène Delacroix	Orientalism - Eugène Delacroix - Eugène Delacroix's orientalism, capturing the exotic and mysterious allure of the East. --v 6.0
Photomontage	Hannah Höch	Photomontage - Hannah Höch - Hannah Höch's groundbreaking photomontage, a feminist exploration of identity and society. --v 6.0

(*continued*)

Style	Artist	Midjourney v 6.0 prompt to demonstrate the style
Photorealistic Sculpture	Duane Hanson	Photorealistic Sculpture - Duane Hanson - Duane Hanson's photorealistic sculpture, ordinary people immortalized with astonishing detail. --v 6.0
Pointillist Painter	Georges Seurat	Pointillist Painter - Georges Seurat - Georges Seurat, a pointillist painter, known for creating images using tiny dots of color. --v 6.0
Pop Art Innovator	Andy Warhol	Pop Art Innovator - Andy Warhol - Andy Warhol, a pop art innovator, transformed everyday objects into art icons. --v 6.0
Pop Surrealism	Mark Ryden	Pop Surrealism - Mark Ryden - Mark Ryden's pop surrealism, blending pop culture references with dreamlike and whimsical imagery. --v 6.0
Post-Impressionism	Paul Cézanne	Post-Impressionism - Paul Cézanne - Paul Cézanne's post-impressionist landscapes, transforming nature into geometric forms and vibrant colors. --v 6.0
Post-Impressionist	Vincent van Gogh	Post-Impressionist - Vincent van Gogh - Vincent van Gogh, a post-impressionist, expressed emotion and movement through bold brushwork and color. --v 6.0
Post-Minimalism	Richard Serra	Post-Minimalism - Richard Serra - Richard Serra's post-minimalist sculpture, monumental forms that challenge space and perception. --v 6.0

(continued)

Style	Artist	Midjourney v 6.0 prompt to demonstrate the style
Precisionism	Charles Demuth	Precisionism - Charles Demuth - Charles Demuth's precisionist painting, celebrating the geometric beauty of American industrial landscapes. --v 6.0
Precisionist Collage	Hannah Höch	Precisionist Collage - Hannah Höch - Hannah Höch's precisionist collage, a feminist deconstruction of society through fragmented images. --v 6.0
Precisionist Painter	Charles Demuth	Precisionist Painter - Charles Demuth - Charles Demuth, a precisionist painter, celebrated the beauty of industrial landscapes with precision. --v 6.0
Precisionist Realism	Charles Demuth	Precisionist Realism - Charles Demuth - Charles Demuth's precisionist realism, capturing the beauty of industrial America with exacting detail. --v 6.0
Precisionist Sculpture	Charles Sheeler	Precisionist Sculpture - Charles Sheeler - Charles Sheeler's precisionist sculpture, combining industrial precision with artistic expression. --v 6.0
Realism	Gustave Courbet	Realism - Gustave Courbet - Gustave Courbet's realism, an honest portrayal of everyday life and the human condition. --v 6.0

(*continued*)

204

Style	Artist	Midjourney v 6.0 prompt to demonstrate the style
Realist Painter	Gustave Courbet	Realist Painter - Gustave Courbet - Gustave Courbet, a realist painter, portrayed everyday life with unfiltered honesty. --v 6.0
Realist Sculpture	Ron van der Werf	Realist Sculpture - Ron van der Werf - Ron van der Werf's realist sculpture, capturing the essence of the human form with precision. --v 6.0
Renaissance	Sandro Botticelli	Renaissance - Sandro Botticelli - Sandro Botticelli's renaissance painting, embodying the grace and beauty of classical antiquity. --v 6.0
Renaissance Icon	Sandro Botticelli	Renaissance Icon - Sandro Botticelli - Sandro Botticelli, a Renaissance icon, portrayed grace and beauty in classical settings. --v 6.0
Renaissance Innovator	Leonardo da Vinci	Renaissance Innovator - Leonardo da Vinci - Leonardo da Vinci, a Renaissance innovator, combined art and science in his iconic works. --v 6.0
Renaissance Innovator	Titian	Renaissance Innovator - Titian - Titian, a Renaissance innovator, used color and texture to create vibrant and sensuous paintings. --v 6.0

(continued)

Style	Artist	Midjourney v 6.0 prompt to demonstrate the style
Renaissance Master	Raphael	Renaissance Master - Raphael - Raphael, a Renaissance master, celebrated for his harmonious and timeless compositions. --v 6.0
Rococo	Jean-Honoré Fragonard	Rococo - Jean-Honoré Fragonard - Jean-Honoré Fragonard's rococo painting, a celebration of frivolity and romance in the 18th century. --v 6.0
Romantic Landscape Artist	John Constable	Romantic Landscape Artist - John Constable - John Constable, a romantic landscape artist, captured the beauty of the English countryside. --v 6.0
Romantic Landscape Painting	J.M.W. Turner	Romantic Landscape Painting - J.M.W. Turner - J.M.W. Turner's romantic landscape painting, harnessing the power and majesty of nature. --v 6.0
Romantic Realism	John Constable	Romantic Realism - John Constable - John Constable's romantic realism, capturing the serene beauty of the English countryside. --v 6.0
Romantic Realist	John Everett Millais	Romantic Realist - John Everett Millais - John Everett Millais, a romantic realist, captured the beauty of nature with meticulous detail. --v 6.0

(*continued*)

Style	Artist	Midjourney v 6.0 prompt to demonstrate the style
Romantic Visionary	William Blake	Romantic Visionary - William Blake - William Blake, a romantic visionary, explored mysticism and imagination in his intricate art. --v 6.0
Romanticism	Caspar David Friedrich	Romanticism - Caspar David Friedrich - Caspar David Friedrich's romantic landscape, conveying the sublime beauty of nature and the human spirit. --v 6.0
Social Realism	Diego Rivera	Social Realism - Diego Rivera - Diego Rivera's social realism, powerful murals depicting social and political themes. --v 6.0
Street Photography	Henri Cartier-Bresson	Street Photography - Henri Cartier-Bresson - Henri Cartier-Bresson's iconic street photography, capturing fleeting moments of everyday life with precision. --v 6.0
Suprematism	Kazimir Malevich	Suprematism - Kazimir Malevich - Kazimir Malevich's iconic suprematist composition featuring simple geometric shapes in a monochromatic masterpiece. --v 6.0
Suprematist Sculpture	El Lissitzky	Suprematist Sculpture - El Lissitzky - El Lissitzky's suprematist sculpture, pushing the boundaries of abstraction and space. --v 6.0

(continued)

Style	Artist	Midjourney v 6.0 prompt to demonstrate the style
Surrealist Photography	Man Ray	Surrealist Photography - Man Ray - Man Ray's surrealist photography, exploring the enigmatic and dreamlike realms of the subconscious. --v 6.0
Surrealist Sculpture	Salvador Dalí	Surrealist Sculpture - Salvador Dalí - Salvador Dalí's surrealist sculpture, a whimsical and surreal exploration of form and meaning. --v 6.0
Symbolic Realism	Lucian Freud	Symbolic Realism - Lucian Freud - Lucian Freud's symbolic realism, intimate and unflinching portraits revealing the human psyche. --v 6.0
Symbolism	Gustav Klimt	Symbolism - Gustav Klimt - Gustav Klimt's symbolic artwork, rich in ornate details and intricate patterns, often exploring themes of love and mysticism. --v 6.0
Symbolist Master	Odilon Redon	Symbolist Master - Odilon Redon - Odilon Redon, a symbolist master, explored the mysterious and dreamlike in his art. --v 6.0
Symbolist Painter	Gustav Klimt	Symbolist Painter - Gustav Klimt - Gustav Klimt, a symbolist painter, infused his art with rich symbolism and ornate patterns. --v 6.0

(*continued*)

Style	Artist	Midjourney v 6.0 prompt to demonstrate the style
Symbolist Sculpture	Auguste Rodin	Symbolist Sculpture - Auguste Rodin - Auguste Rodin's symbolist sculpture, conveying complex emotions and human experiences. --v 6.0
Synchromism	Morgan Russell	Synchromism - Morgan Russell - Morgan Russell's synchromism, a visual symphony of color and form in abstract compositions. --v 6.0
Tachisme	Pierre Soulages	Tachisme - Pierre Soulages - Pierre Soulages' abstract tachisme painting, where bold brushstrokes and gestural marks take center stage. --v 6.0
Tachist Sculpture	Antoni Tàpies	Tachist Sculpture - Antoni Tàpies - Antoni Tàpies' tachist sculpture, where texture and materials take center stage in abstract forms. --v 6.0
Tonalism	James McNeill Whistler	Tonalism - James McNeill Whistler - James McNeill Whistler's tonalist painting, evoking a sense of poetic tranquility through subtle shades of color. --v 6.0
Transgressive Art	Chris Ofili	Transgressive Art - Chris Ofili - Chris Ofili's transgressive art, provocative and unconventional explorations of identity and culture. --v 6.0
Visionary Art	Alex Grey	Visionary Art - Alex Grey - Alex Grey's visionary art, a spiritual journey through intricate and cosmic realms. --v 6.0

APPENDIX D

Goblincore and Others: Midjourney's Vocabulary

This list was shared on Reddit with the attribution to David Holz, the CEO of Midjourney, a while ago. But in fact, you can combine any word ending in -core, -punk, or -wave, and it would make sense to Midjourney.

© The Editor(s) (if applicable) and The Author(s),
under exclusive license to APress Media, LLC, part of Springer Nature 2024
I. Shamaeva, *Advanced Styles and Insights with Midjourney*,
https://doi.org/10.1007/979-8-8688-0336-9

aetherclockpunk	cosmicpunk	librarypunk	priestpunk	slimepunk	steampunk	synthpunk
aetherpunk	crackpunk	limbpunk	princepunk	steelpunk	steempunk	technopunk
algeapunk	craterpunk	limpcore	princesspunk	stonepunk	steelpunk	techpunk
alienpunk	crustpunk	lorespunk	princelingpunk	swordpunk	synthpunk	vaporpunk
atompunk	cryptopunk	magicpunk	punk	syndicatepunk	technopunk	xmaspunk
aurorapunk	cyberaetherpunk	manapunk	queerpunk	synthpunk	techpunk	zuckerpunk
autopunk	cybermysticpunk	mcdonaldpunk	ragpunk	technopunk	vaporpunk	bibliopunk
avocadopunk	cybermysticsteampunk	meatpunk	ragepunk	techpunk	xmaspunk	bronzepunk
avocadopunk	cyberpunk	necropunk	ravepunk	technopunk	zuckerpunk	cargopunk
berrypunk	cyberpunkpunk	neonpunk	raypunk	techpunk	bibliopunk	corporatepunk
biopunk	cyberraypunk	neopunk	redpunk	technopunk	bronzepunk	cripplepunk
carpetpunk	cybersteampunk	pantonepunk	regencypunk	technopunk	cargopunk	cyberneticpunk
celestialpunk	cyperpunk	pencilsteampunk	retropunk	techpunk	cargopunk	daydreampunk
chinapunk	cypherpunk	piratepunk	rockpunk	technopunk	corporatepunk	dinopunk
chromepunk	decopunk	poodlepunk	roguepunk	techpunk	cripplepunk	dracopunk

chronopunk	derppunk	postpunk	rollpunk	technopunk	cyberneticpunk	europunk
citypunk	desertpunk	psychedelicpunk	safepunk	technopunk	daydreampunk	folk punk
clockpunk	dieselpunk	punk	samuraipunk	technopunk	dinopunk	forestpunk
cloudpunk	diselpunk	quantumpunk	savagepunk	technopunk	dracopunk	gadgetpunk
clownpunk	draftpunk	ragepunk	scalypunk	technopunk	europunk	hermitpunk
coralpunk	dreampunk	seapunk	schoolpunk	technopunk	folk punk	lunarpunk
cottagepunk	fantasypunk	sithpunk	scifipunk	technopunk	forestpunk	mythpunk
crustpunk	fiberpunk	slaughterpunk	shadowpunk	technopunk	gadgetpunk	nanopunk
cryptopunk	fibrepunk	solapunk	sharkpunk	technopunk	hermitpunk	pastel punk
cyberaetherpunk	floralpunk	solarpunk	shockpunk	technopunk	lunarpunk	post-punk
cybermysticpunk	flowerpunk	spacepunk	shrinkpunk	technopunk	mythpunk	salvagepunk
cybermysticsteampunk	foampunk	spacesolarpunk	skunkpunk	technopunk	nanopunk	sandalpunk
cyberpunk	fractalpunk	starpunk	sleepypunk	technopunk	pastel punk	slimepunk
cyberpunkpunk	frostpunk	steampunk	smallpunk	technopunk	post-punk	steelpunk
cyberraypunk	futurepunk	steempunk	smashpunk	technopunk	salvagepunk	stonepunk
cybersteampunk	genepunk	synthpunk	smirkpunk	technopunk	sandalpunk	swordpunk

(continued)

bibliopunk	slimepunk	technopunk	snailpunk	technopunk	geopunk	cyperpunk
bronzepunk	steampunk	technopunk	sneakerpunk	techpunk	ghoulpunk	cypherpunk
cargopunk	steempunk	technopunk	snowpunk	vaporpunk	glitchpunk	decopunk
corporate punk	synthpunk	technopunk	sockpunk	xmaspunk	goosepunk	derppunk
cyberneticpunk	vaporpunk	technopunk	solarpunk	zuckerpunk	gothicpunk	desertpunk
cripplepunk	xmaspunk	technopunk	songpunk	bibliopunk	icepunk	dieselpunk
daydreampunk	zuckerpunk	technopunk	spacepunk	bronzepunk	industrialpunk	diselpunk
dinopunk	vaporpunk	technopunk	starpunk	cargopunk	junglepunk	draftpunk
dracopunk	xmaspunk	technopunk	steampunk	corporate punk	kawaiipunk	dreampunk
europunk	bibliopunk	technopunk	steempunk	cripplepunk	kombuchapunk	fantasypunk
folk punk	cargopunk	technopunk	synthpunk	cyberneticpunk	magipunk	fiberpunk
forestpunk	cyberneticpunk	technopunk	vaporpunk	daydreampunk	manapunk	fibrepunk
				dinopunk	mcdonaldpunk	floralpunk

APPENDIX E

Strong Modifiers

These expressive words, which we can call modifiers or qualifiers, will strongly influence your images' styles.

- Vintage, retro, classic

- Modern, contemporary, futuristic

- Expressive, emotive, dramatic

- Conceptual, interpretive, metaphorical

- Cartoonish, animated, caricatured

- Monochromatic, grayscale, sepia

- Glossy, polished, sleek

- Rustic, earthy, natural

- Urban, gritty, street-style

- Experimental, avant-garde, unconventional

- Digital, pixelated, binary

- Hand-drawn, sketched, illustrated

- Collage, mixed-media, composite

- Geometric, linear, angular

- Organic, naturalistic, lifelike
- Textured, detailed, intricate
- Bold, vibrant, colorful
- Subtle, muted, pastel
- Dark, moody, atmospheric
- Light, airy, ethereal
- Narrative, storytelling, cinematic
- Dreamlike, fantastical, mythical
- Historical, period-specific, antiquated
- Minimalist, clean, sparse
- Ornate, baroque, embellished
- Kinetic, dynamic, flowing
- Static, still, unmoving
- Architectural, structural, built
- Fluid, liquid, aqueous
- Crystalline, geometric, faceted
- Organic, biomorphic, curvilinear
- Symbolist, allegorical, emblematic
- Cosmic, stellar, celestial
- Underwater, marine, aquatic
- Aerial, atmospheric, sky-bound
- Arctic, glacial, icy
- Desert, arid, sandy

- Forest, wooded, leafy

- Mountainous, rocky, rugged

- Urban, cityscape, metropolitan

- Rural, pastoral, bucolic

- Industrial, mechanical, technological

- Cubist, fragmented, Picasso-like

- Impressionist, light-focused, Monet-inspired

- Realist, lifelike, Vermeer-type

- Abstract expressionist, gestural, Pollock-like

- Minimalist, reductive, Rothko-style

- Futurist, dynamic, Boccioni-influenced

- Romantic, emotive, Turner-esque

- Gothic, dark, mysterious

- Baroque, dramatic, Caravaggio-like

- Renaissance, balanced, Da Vinci-style

- Pre-Raphaelite, detailed, Waterhouse-inspired

- Neoclassical, formal, David-like

- Rococo, ornate, Fragonard-esque

- Byzantine, mosaic, iconographic

- Art Nouveau, flowing, Mucha-influenced

- Art Deco, geometric, streamlined

- Op Art, optical, Vasarely-like

- Pop Art, bold, Warhol-style

- Street art, graffiti, Banksy-like

- Photomontage, layered, Höch-inspired

- Conceptual art, idea-driven, Duchamp-esque

- Performance, live, Abramović-like

- Installation, immersive, Hirst-style

- Video art, multimedia, Paik-influenced

- Sound art, auditory, Cage-like

- Earthworks, land art, Smithson-style

- Body art, corporeal, Orlan-esque

- Digital art, virtual, interactive

- Generative art, algorithmic, computer-created

- Bio art, living, Kac-like

- Eco art, environmental, sustainable

- Social practice, community-focused, participatory

- Relational aesthetics, interactive, Bourriaud-influenced

- Outsider art, self-taught, folk

- Brutalist, raw, concrete

- Abstract, non-representational, form-focused

- Kinetic, moving, Calder-like

- Light and space, perceptual, Turrell-inspired

- Pattern and decoration, ornamental, celebratory

- Feminist art, gender-focused, Chicago-like

- Postmodern, eclectic, Koons-style

- Neo-expressionist, intense, Basquiat-influenced

- Neo-geo, geometric abstraction, minimalist

- Hyperrealist, high-detail, Close-like

- Surrealist, dreamlike, Magritte-style

- Psychedelic, hallucinatory, vivid

- Trompe-l'oeil, illusionistic, realistic

- Narrative, story-telling, illustrative

- Figurative, representational, human-focused

- Abstract figuration, distorted, Bacon-like

- Color field, color as subject, Newman-esque

- Hard-edge, sharp boundaries, Hockney-style

- Constructivist, geometric, Rodchenko-like

- Suprematism, abstract, Malevich-inspired

- Dada, anti-art, random, Duchamp-like

- Fluxus, experimental, intermedia

- Arte Povera, raw materials, non-traditional

- Neo-Dada, postwar, Rauschenberg-inspired

- Process art, method-focused, procedural

- Land art, environmental, large-scale

- Net art, internet-based, digital

- New media art, technology-driven, interactive

- Conceptual photography, idea-based, staged

- Documentary photography, reality-focused, candid

- Portrait photography, individual-focused, expressive

- Landscape photography, nature-focused, scenic

- Street photography, urban, spontaneous

- Fine art photography, artistic, composed

- Photojournalism, news-focused, informative

- Architectural photography, structure-focused, detailed

- Fashion photography, style-focused, glamorous

- Sports photography, action-focused, dynamic

- Wildlife photography, animal-focused, natural

- Astrophotography, space-focused, celestial

- Macro photography, close-up, detailed

- Aerial photography, bird's-eye view, expansive

- Underwater photography, aquatic, submerged

- Travel photography, culture-focused, exploratory

- Food photography, culinary, appetizing

- Still life photography, object-focused, composed

APPENDIX F

Two-Color Combinations

Images drawn in two complementary colors are often aesthetically pleasant.

- Lavender and Sage Green
- Lime Green and Plum
- Marigold and Slate Blue
- Tangerine and Aqua
- Fuchsia and Sea Green
- Dusty Rose and Navy Blue
- Mint Green and Raspberry
- Lemon Yellow and Lavender
- Scarlet and Olive Green
- Emerald and Burnt Orange
- Peach and Periwinkle
- Lilac and Silver

© The Editor(s) (if applicable) and The Author(s),
under exclusive license to APress Media, LLC, part of Springer Nature 2024
I. Shamaeva, *Advanced Styles and Insights with Midjourney*,
https://doi.org/10.1007/979-8-8688-0336-9

- Goldenrod and Sky Blue

- Amber and Indigo

- Royal Blue and Melon

- Blush Pink and Forest Green

- Dandelion Yellow and Mulberry

- Crimson and Cyan

- Cherry Red and Teal Green

- Coral and Turquoise

- Turquoise Blue and Warm Beige

- Electric Blue and Gold

- Neon Pink and Charcoal Gray

- Violet and Lemon Green

- Midnight Blue and Pumpkin Orange

- Powder Blue and Peach Orange

- Ruby Red and Mint Blue

- Chartreuse and Magenta

- Teal and Coral Pink

- Cobalt Blue and Tangerine Orange

- Cerulean and Saffron Yellow

- Aquamarine and Cherry Blossom Pink

- Ultramarine and Gold Ochre

- Pistachio and Burgundy

- Sapphire and Sunflower Yellow

- Jade Green and Blush Red

- Indigo Blue and Neon Green

- Raspberry Pink and Lime Green

- Olive Green and Bright Pink

APPENDIX G

References and Resources

- Midjourney Documentation – `https://docs.midjourney.com`

- Midjourney Quick Start Guide – `https://docs.midjourney.com/docs/quick-start`

- Midjourney Prompt FAQs (you need to be logged into Discord and be a Midjourney member) – `https://discord.com/channels/662267976984297473/1017917091606712430`

- Aesthetics Wiki – `https://aesthetics.fandom.com/wiki/List_of_Aesthetics`

- Midlibrary – `https://midlibrary.io/`. An advanced library of genres, artistic movements, techniques, titles, and artists' styles for Midjourney AI

- Facebook Group "Midjourney Images & Insights. Share, Discuss Your Best Creations, Prompts" – `www.facebook.com/groups/ourbestmidjourneyimages` (I am one of the Admins. Our group has regular challenges, contests, and artist highlights.)

- AI artists to follow:

    - Jade Jenerai (Joyce Ling) – `www.facebook.com/jadejenerai`

    - John Weber – `www.facebook.com/groups/777337440666020/user/100011032862489`

    - Valerija Mezhybovska – `www.facebook.com/lerusisikai`

    - Mike Ososky – `www.facebook.com/profile.php?id=100092099323180`

- My Facebook portfolio – `www.facebook.com/aibraingain`

- My website – `www.theprompter.com`

Index

© The Editor(s) (if applicable) and The Author(s),
under exclusive license to APress Media, LLC, part of Springer Nature 2024
I. Shamaeva, *Advanced Styles and Insights with Midjourney*,
https://doi.org/10.1007/979-8-8688-0336-9

227

GPSR Compliance
The European Union's (EU) General Product Safety Regulation (GPSR) is a set
of rules that requires consumer products to be safe and our obligations to
ensure this.

If you have any concerns about our products, you can contact us on

ProductSafety@springernature.com

In case Publisher is established outside the EU, the EU authorized
representative is:

Springer Nature Customer Service Center GmbH
Europaplatz 3
69115 Heidelberg, Germany